Great Sedona Hikes

REVISED FIFTH

AN EASY-TO-USE GUIDE
FOR OVER 100 HIKING TRAILS and
LOOP HIKES IN SEDONA, ARIZONA

FEATURING OUR
20 FAVORITE HIKING TRAILS
and LOOP HIKES

William Bohan

and

David Butler

Non-liability Statement

The authors have taken every precaution to ensure that the information contained within is up-to-date, accurate and reflects trail conditions when this guide was printed. However, trail conditions frequently change because of weather, Forest Service activity or other causes. The GPS data included were obtained from a Garmin model 60CSx GPS unit. Because the data are only as accurate as the sensitivity of the GPS unit, some inaccuracies may be present. Users of GPS data are urged to use common sense when hiking. Always stay on the trail. The authors, publisher, contributors, and all those involved in the preparation of this guide, either directly or indirectly, disclaim any liability for injuries, accidents, and damages whatsoever that may occur to those using this guide. You are responsible for your health and safety while hiking the trails.

Acknowledgments

The authors would like to acknowledge several individuals for their contributions to this guide. They are:

Ruth Butler, Lorna Thompson and Nancy Williams for their efforts in editing this work; Brenda Andrusyszyn, Michelle Barrett, Wade Bell, Carole Bell, Barbara Lewis, Jim Rostedt, Kathy Rostedt, Gary Stouder, Barrie Thomas, Grace Thomas, Darryl Thompson, Lorna Thompson and Marjorie Whitton for their companionship while hiking the trails.

ISBN-13: 978-1986388764
ISBN-10: 198638876X

Front Cover Photo: Bear Mountain Trail

Table of Contents

Changes to This Edition

In this Fifth Edition, we added 25 additional trails including Skywalker and Rector Connector plus a number of loop hikes. Individual descriptions, photos and trail maps have been updated where necessary to the latest trail conditions.

QR Code Technology

Because of space limitations, we are able to include only one representative black and white photograph from each trail in this guide. But using mobile device technology, you can scan the QR Code found near each trail map which will give you access to additional color photos of that trail.

Cumulative Ascent Definition

The reader will notice that the maps contain cumulative ascent data. Elevation change simply reflects the difference between the lowest and highest elevations of the trail. Cumulative ascent reflects the ups and downs of the trail and is always greater than elevation change.

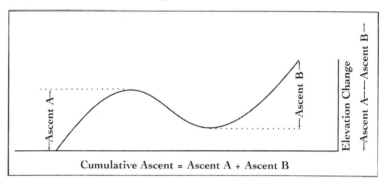

Hiking Time

Hiking time is estimated based on a hiking speed of between 1.5 and 2 miles per hour. Trails that have a large cumulative ascent are at the lower end of that range to allow for stops to catch your breath. Hiking time does not include stops for snacks, photographs, meditation, etc.

Trail Popularity

The popularity of each trail is indicated by symbols (🚶🚶🚶🚶 for a very popular trail and 🚶 for a trail that isn't used very often). You should expect crowds on trails with 4 hiker symbols and likely won't encounter other hikers on a trail that has just one hiker symbol. Weekends in Sedona tend to result in more hikers on the trails and holidays can be especially busy.

In-Out Hikes vs. Loop Hikes

For an in-out hike, you'll hike a trail for a distance then retrace your steps to return to the parking area. A loop hike is a circular hike using either a single trail (e.g. Baldwin Trail) or a combination of several trails and you essentially will not retrace your steps to return to the parking area.

Safe Hiking Tips

The stunning red rock formations, moderate temperatures and close proximity to the trails make hiking in Sedona an experience unlike anywhere else in the world. But hiking is not without risk. It is very important to be prepared, even for a day hike. Bring enough water to stay hydrated and drink water throughout the hike. In addition:

- Check the weather before you begin hiking and reschedule your hike if inclement weather is predicted
- Wear a hat and sunscreen and take along a wind breaker or light raincoat
- Hiking poles may help with balance on the uneven trails
- Wear hiking boots or sturdy walking shoes with good grip as the trails can be uneven and rocky
- Carry a first-aid kit, a fully charged cell phone (although many hiking trails do not have cell phone service), flashlight, compass, hiking guide, map, portable GPS unit, rescue whistle, pocketknife and a snack
- Hike with at least one other person and complete the hike before sunset
- If you must hike alone, let someone know where you'll be hiking and leave a note in your vehicle stating where you intend to hike and when you expect to return
- Trailhead parking areas can be the target of thieves so don't leave valuables in your vehicle
- Stay on the designated trail. Most rescues are for hikers who have left the trail to "explore"
- Downhill hikers have the right-of-way in most instances because footing is more tenuous downhill than uphill. If hiking uphill, step aside and let downhill hikers pass
- Bicyclists are supposed to yield to all trail users, but use common sense and step aside when appropriate
- There is no trash service in the forest. Take out anything you take in. "Take nothing but pictures, leave nothing but footprints"

Definition of the "Y"

If you obtain directions from a Sedona local, chances are he or she will give you those directions referencing something called the "Y." We use the "Y" as our reference point in this guidebook also. The "Y" is the traffic circle at the intersection of State Route (SR) 89A and SR 179.

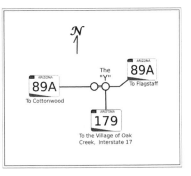

If you drive to Sedona from Flagstaff on SR 89A, the "Y" is the first of the two roundabouts you come to. And, if you drive to Sedona from Cottonwood, the "Y" is the second roundabout you enter, which is very close to the first roundabout.

5

Aerie Trail

Summary: An in-out hike across the north side of Doe Mountain with excellent views of Doe Mountain, Bear Mountain, Fay Canyon and Boynton Canyon

Challenge Level:
Moderate

Hiking Distance: 2.9 miles each way from the Aerie parking area to the Boynton Canyon parking area or 5.8 miles round trip

Hiking Time: About 3 hours round trip

Trail Popularity:

Trailhead Directions: From the "Y" roundabout (see page 5), drive west toward Cottonwood on SR 89A about 3 miles. Turn right onto Dry Creek Road (where speed limits are strictly enforced). Stay on Dry Creek Road to a stop sign (about 3 miles) then turn left onto Boynton Pass Road. Proceed about 1.6 miles to a stop sign. Turn left and continue on Boynton Pass Road. Drive about 2.5 miles then turn left onto Aerie Road, which is about 0.5 mile past the Doe Mountain/Bear Mountain parking area on the left side of Boynton Pass Road. Follow Aerie Road and take the right fork to the parking area {1}.

Description: The trail begins near the signboard at the west end of the parking lot. About 100 feet south of the parking area is a trail sign. Turn left (east) to hike the Aerie Trail across the north side of Doe Mountain all the way to the Boynton Canyon parking area. The best views are along the north side of Doe Mountain on the Aerie Trail.

If you follow the Aerie Trail from the parking area, you'll cross Aerie Drive, which leads to the Aerie Subdivision, then you'll come to the Doe Mountain Trail {2} after 0.8 mile. The Aerie Trail takes a slight jog here at the intersection with the Doe Mountain Trail but is well-marked. You'll bend to the right then to the left as you hike around the northeast side of Doe Mountain. Next you'll intersect the Cockscomb Trail {3} after 2.5 miles then cross Boynton Canyon Road {4} on your 2.9 mile hike to the Boynton Canyon parking area {5}.

You'll have excellent views of Doe Mountain, Bear Mountain, Fay Canyon and Boynton Canyon. You may encounter some mountain bikers on the trail as you hike toward and return from the Boynton Canyon Trail parking area. The Boynton Canyon Trail parking area has a toilet.

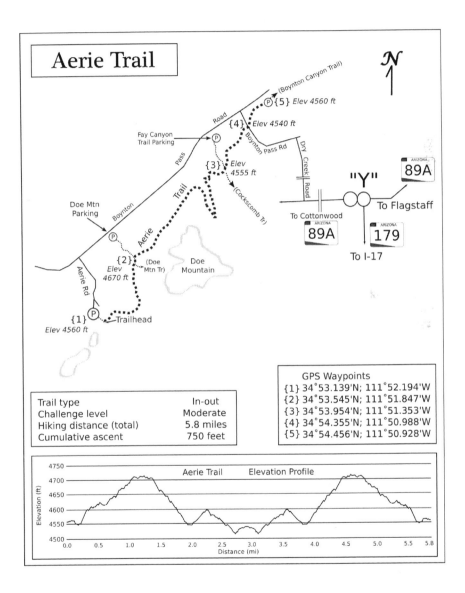

Aerie Trail

(Boynton Canyon Trail)

N

P {5} *Elev 4560 ft*

{4} *Elev 4540 ft*

Road

Fay Canyon
Trail Parking

Boynton Pass Rd

Dry Creek Road

"Y"

89A

{3} *Elev 4555 ft*

Pass

Trail

(Cockscomb Tr)

To Flagstaff

To Cottonwood

Doe Mtn
Parking

Boynton

89A

179

Aerie

P

{2} *Elev 4670 ft*

(Doe Mtn Tr)

Doe
Mountain

To I-17

Aerie Rd

{1} P Trailhead
Elev 4560 ft

Trail type	In-out
Challenge level	Moderate
Hiking distance (total)	5.8 miles
Cumulative ascent	750 feet

GPS Waypoints
{1} 34°53.139'N; 111°52.194'W
{2} 34°53.545'N; 111°51.847'W
{3} 34°53.954'N; 111°51.353'W
{4} 34°54.355'N; 111°50.988'W
{5} 34°54.456'N; 111°50.928'W

Aerie Trail   Elevation Profile

Elevation (ft)

Distance (mi)

Airport Loop and Airport Vortex

Summary: A loop hike that circles the Sedona Airport with nice views all around and a chance to visit one of Sedona's famous vortexes

Challenge Level: Easy for the vortex hike; Moderate for the loop hike

Hiking Distance: From the Airport Road parking area {1} less than 0.25 mile round trip for the vortex; about 3.3 miles for the loop hike, but add another 1 mile if you hike the Tabletop Trail. Add 1.2 miles to all the above mileages if you hike from the Sedona View parking area {2}.

Hiking Time: From the Airport Road parking area, about ½ hour round trip for the vortex; about 2 hours for the loop: add ½ hour for the Tabletop Trail. From the Sedona View parking area, add 1 hour to the above estimated hiking times.

Trail Popularity: For the vortex: 🚶🚶🚶🚶 For the loop hike: 🚶🚶

Trailhead Directions: There are two ways to access this trail. From the "Y" roundabout (see page 5), drive west toward Cottonwood on SR 89A for 1 mile then turn left onto Airport Road, which is the first traffic light west of the "Y." The primary trailhead is located approximately 0.5 mile up Airport Road on the left {1}. There is parking for 10 vehicles plus one handicapped spot here.

If the parking lot is full, continue on for 0.6 mile then turn left into the Scenic Overlook parking area. The Sedona View trailhead is at the northeast corner of the parking area {2}. Note: there is a $3 parking fee at the Scenic Overlook parking area.

Description: If you park on Airport Road {1}, you can easily reach one of Sedona's famous vortexes. From the parking area continue past the first sign then follow the main trail east until you come to a second sign in about 200 feet {3}. Turn left here then follow the trail to Overlook Point for a short distance then make a right turn to climb up about 50 feet to the overlook. The top of the rock formation is Overlook Point and is considered to be the vortex {4}. (Additional information on vortexes can be found on page 144.) From the Scenic View parking area {2}, hike the Sedona View Trail downhill for 0.6 mile. You'll probably see people atop the Airport Vortex ahead. Continue past the intersection with the Airport Loop Trail to the intersection with the sign for Overlook Point {3} to go to the vortex {4}.

As you hike around Airport Mesa below the Sedona Airport, there are good views all around. On the east, there are great views of Twin Buttes and, to the south, Cathedral Rock. Be sure to hike the 0.5 mile Tabletop Trail at the southwest end of the runway {5} to the end of the mesa {6} for a spectacular view of Sedona's Pyramid. Return to the Airport Loop Trail where after 0.6 mile you'll intersect the Bandit Trail {7} and have nice views of Chimney Rock, Capitol Butte and Coffeepot Rock on the north side of the loop.

Note: Don't attempt this rock-strewn trail if a narrow trail and steep drop-offs are a concern. The trail is very rocky and twisted ankles are a common occurrence.

Color Photos: Scan the QR code for color photos of this trail

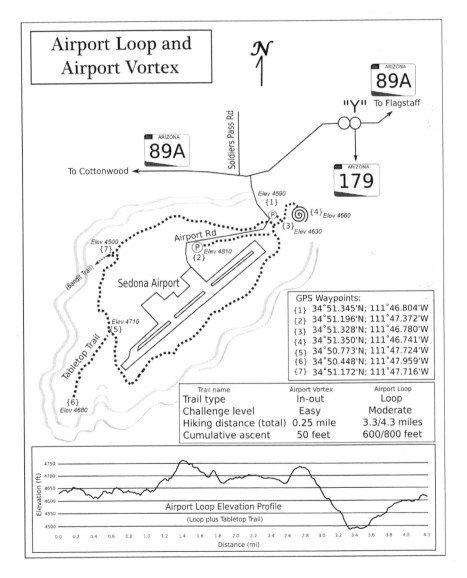

Airport Loop and Airport Vortex

Trail name	Airport Vortex	Airport Loop
Trail type	In-out	Loop
Challenge level	Easy	Moderate
Hiking distance (total)	0.25 mile	3.3/4.3 miles
Cumulative ascent	50 feet	600/800 feet

GPS Waypoints:
{1} 34°51.345'N; 111°46.804'W
{2} 34°51.196'N; 111°47.372'W
{3} 34°51.328'N; 111°46.780'W
{4} 34°51.350'N; 111°46.741'W
{5} 34°50.773'N; 111°47.724'W
{6} 34°50.448'N; 111°47.959'W
{7} 34°51.172'N; 111°47.716'W

Airport Loop Elevation Profile
(Loop plus Tabletop Trail)

Baldwin Loop ★

Summary: This loop trail at the base of Cathedral Rock offers some excellent views with an optional short side trip to the banks of Oak Creek

Challenge Level:
Moderate

Hiking Distance: About a 2.7 mile loop

Hiking Time: About 1½ hours round trip

Trail Popularity:

Trailhead Directions:
The trailhead is located on the unpaved portion of Verde Valley School Road. From the "Y" roundabout (see page 5), drive south on SR 179 about 7 miles to the Jacks Canyon and Verde Valley School Road roundabout then turn right (west) onto Verde Valley School Road. At 4 miles you'll pass the Turkey Creek parking area on your left {10} and at 4.5 miles you'll see the Baldwin Trail parking area on the left (west) side of Verde Valley School Road {1}. The trailhead is across the road from the north end of the parking area. There are toilets at the parking area.

Description: Named for Andrew Baldwin, one of the individuals who bought Crescent Moon Ranch in 1936, the Baldwin Loop Trail circles an unnamed red rock butte beside Cathedral Rock providing excellent panoramic views of Cathedral Rock. After crossing the road, you'll come to a signboard {2}. You can hike the Baldwin Trail in either direction. If you hike in the clockwise direction, you'll intersect an unmarked "social trail" in 0.3 mile {3} and the Templeton Trail after 0.5 mile {4}. Take a side trip by hiking east on the Templeton Trail until it goes beside Oak Creek. After 0.2 mile, look across Oak Creek to see Buddha Beach, where visitors use river rock to build amazing stacked structures {5}. Periodically, floods knock the structures down, but they are usually quickly rebuilt. You may be lucky and see hundreds of buddhas. If you continue east on the Templeton Trail for 0.8 mile, you'll intersect the Cathedral Rock Trail.

Return to the Baldwin Loop Trail intersection then turn left to continue around the tall red rock butte. You'll pass some excellent places to stop and enjoy the views {6}{8} on your loop. You'll intersect the HiLine Trail {7}, which is a popular mountain biking trail, and a spur off of the Baldwin Loop Trail {9} that leads across Verde Valley School Road to the Turkey Creek Trail parking area {10}. For the best photos of Cathedral Rock, do this hike later in the day.

Color Photos: Scan the QR code for color photos of this trail

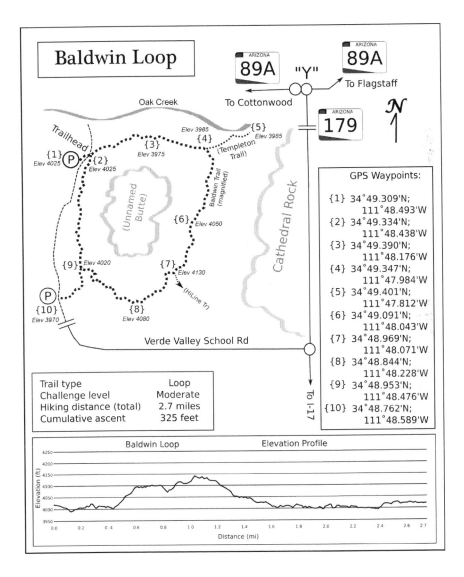

Baldwin Loop

ARIZONA **89A** "Y" ARIZONA **89A**

To Flagstaff

Oak Creek To Cottonwood

ARIZONA **179**

$\mathcal{N}$

Trailhead

Elev 3985 {5} Elev 3985

{4}

{3} Elev 3975

(Templeton Trail)

{1} P {2}
Elev 4025 Elev 4025

(Unnamed Butte)

Baldwin Trail (magnified)

Cathedral Rock

{6} Elev 4050

{9} Elev 4020 {7} Elev 4130

(HiLine Tr)

P
{10} {8}
Elev 3970 Elev 4080

Verde Valley School Rd

To I-17

Trail type	Loop
Challenge level	Moderate
Hiking distance (total)	2.7 miles
Cumulative ascent	325 feet

GPS Waypoints:

{1} 34°49.309'N; 111°48.493'W
{2} 34°49.334'N; 111°48.438'W
{3} 34°49.390'N; 111°48.176'W
{4} 34°49.347'N; 111°47.984'W
{5} 34°49.401'N; 111°47.812'W
{6} 34°49.091'N; 111°48.043'W
{7} 34°48.969'N; 111°48.071'W
{8} 34°48.844'N; 111°48.228'W
{9} 34°48.953'N; 111°48.476'W
{10} 34°48.762'N; 111°48.589'W

Baldwin Loop Elevation Profile

Elevation (ft) — 4250, 4200, 4150, 4100, 4050, 4000, 3950

Distance (mi) — 0.0 0.2 0.4 0.6 0.8 1.0 1.2 1.4 1.6 1.8 2.0 2.2 2.4 2.6 2.7

Bear Mountain Trail ★

Summary: A strenuous, sunny, in-out hike with excellent red rock views

Challenge Level: Hard

Hiking Distance: About 2.4 miles each way to the top of Bear Mountain or 4.8 miles round trip

Hiking Time: About 4 hours round trip

Trail Popularity: 🚶🚶

Trailhead Directions: From the "Y" roundabout (see page 5), drive west toward Cottonwood on SR 89A about 3 miles. Turn right onto Dry Creek Road (where speed limits are strictly enforced). Stay on Dry Creek Road to a stop sign (about 3 miles) then turn left onto Boynton Pass Road. Proceed about 1.6 miles to a stop sign. Turn left and continue on Boynton Pass Road. The trailhead parking {1} is shared with Doe Mountain Trail and is the second parking area on the left side, about 1.75 miles from the stop sign. The Bear Mountain Trail begins across the road from the parking area. There are toilets at the parking area.

Description: Bear Mountain provides fantastic views of Doe Mountain (and beyond) and nearby canyons. You'll be hiking up with a cumulative ascent of some 2100 feet. This makes Bear Mountain a hard hike.

After crossing the road and stepping over a low fence, you first cross a series of three deep washes and enter a meadow-like landscape. After 0.3 mile, you begin the climb up the mountain. Throughout the hike, be sure to look around to enjoy the great views. After 0.7 mile you'll come to a huge rock beside the trail {2}.

At 1.2 mile you'll come to a flat area {3} and soon have to scramble up in a narrow slot. At 1.4 miles, you'll reach a summit {4} then begin a series of descents and ascents. At 2 miles, you'll come to a large area of slickrock {5}, soon followed by a natural stopping place and photo opportunity at elevation 6150 feet {6}.

To reach the very top of Bear Mountain, you'll hike an additional 0.4 mile with ascents and descents. From the top of Bear Mountain {7}, look north and you can see the San Francisco Peaks northwest of Flagstaff.

Note: The trail is fairly well-marked by white paint markers and cairns placed by other hikers. The trail is rocky with exposed and extreme drop-offs in some parts – watch your footing.

Color Photos: Scan the QR code for color photos of this trail

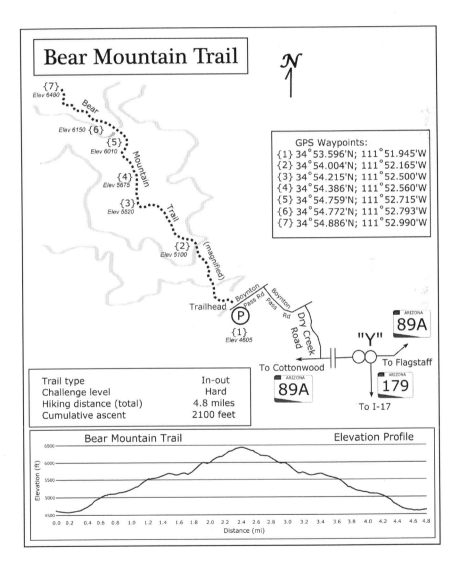

Bear Sign Trail

Summary: A beautiful in-out hike in a forested red rock canyon

Challenge Level:
Moderate

Hiking Distance: About 3 miles each way or 6 miles round trip

Hiking Time: About 4 hours round trip

Trail Popularity:

Trailhead Directions:
From the "Y" roundabout (see page 5), drive west toward Cottonwood on SR 89A about 3 miles. Turn right onto Dry Creek Road (where speed limits are strictly enforced). Stay on Dry Creek Road for 2 miles then turn right onto Forest Road (FR) 152. Proceed to the end of FR 152 (about 4.5 miles) to the parking area on the left {1}. The parking area is the same as used for the Dry Creek and Vultee Arch Trails.

Note: FR 152 is an extremely rough road beyond the 0.2 mile paved section; a high clearance vehicle and 4WD are strongly recommended.

Description: This trail is seldom used because it is difficult to drive to. As a result the trail will likely be somewhat overgrown with logs and other obstacles you must navigate. But the feeling of being alone in the forest, in the wilderness is wonderful. And you'll find many wildflowers at certain times.

After you park, proceed in a northwesterly direction on the Dry Creek Trail. You'll be hiking in the forest so there is shade. The trail is relatively flat at the start then begins a gentle climb. After about 0.6 mile, you'll come to a fork where the Dry Creek Trail goes to the right and the Bear Sign Trail begins to the left {2}. Grizzly bears reportedly roamed the area until the 1930s; you may actually see signs of black bear along the trail.

Hike some 2.8 miles to the intersection of the David Miller Trail {3}. A short, but steep hike up the David Miller Trail about 0.2 mile provides a lovely view from the saddle of the ridge between Bear Sign and Secret Canyons {4}. If you'd like to hike a 6.6 mile loop, see Secret Canyon/Bear Sign Loop.

Color Photos: Scan the QR code for color photos of this trail

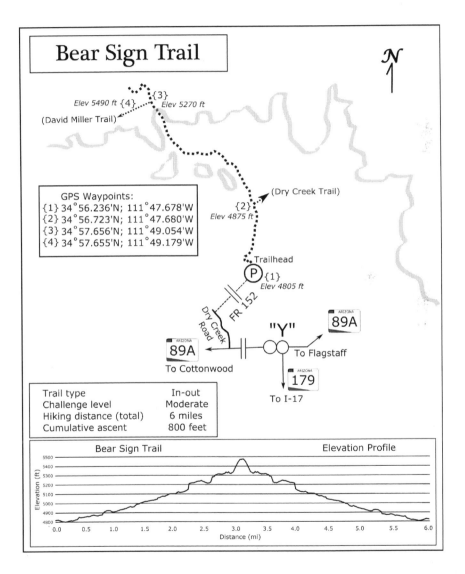

Bear Sign Trail

N

Elev 5490 ft {4}
{3}
Elev 5270 ft
(David Miller Trail)

(Dry Creek Trail)

GPS Waypoints:
{1} 34°56.236'N; 111°47.678'W
{2} 34°56.723'N; 111°47.680'W
{3} 34°57.656'N; 111°49.054'W
{4} 34°57.655'N; 111°49.179'W

{2}
Elev 4875 ft

Trailhead

P {1}
Elev 4805 ft

Dry Creek Road

FR 152

"Y"

ARIZONA
89A

ARIZONA
89A
To Cottonwood

To Flagstaff

ARIZONA
179
To I-17

Trail type	In-out
Challenge level	Moderate
Hiking distance (total)	6 miles
Cumulative ascent	800 feet

Bear Sign Trail   Elevation Profile

15

Bell Rock Climb and Bell Rock Vortex

Summary: Explore a famous Sedona rock formation and perhaps experience some vortex energy

Challenge Level: Easy but watch your footing

Hiking Distance: About 1.2 miles round trip

Hiking Time: About 1 hour round trip

Trail Popularity:

Trailhead Directions: From the "Y" roundabout (see page 5), drive south on SR 179 for about 5 miles to the parking area. After you drive about 3.2 miles, just past the Back O' Beyond roundabout, SR 179 becomes a divided highway. Continue driving south. About 1.8 miles beyond the Back O' Beyond roundabout, southbound SR 179 adds a passing lane on the left. From the passing lane, turn left at the sign for the Court House Vista parking area {1} (it's the second scenic view on the left side of SR 179). Before you turn, you'll see Bell Rock ahead of you on the left side of SR 179. There are toilets at the parking area. The trail starts just beyond the interpretive signboard.

Description: After you park in the Court House Vista parking area, walk past the interpretive signboard then proceed straight ahead on the Bell Rock Trail. Follow it for 0.2 mile to the intersection with the Bell Rock Pathway (BRP) Trail {2}. Continue straight ahead then make a slight left onto the Bell Rock Climb. In about 0.1 mile (and after climbing up about 65 feet), you'll intersect the Rector Connector Trail {3}. Make a right turn then continue to follow Bell Rock Climb and you'll shortly come to a large relatively flat area {4}.

You'll note that Bell Rock Climb goes to the left and right. If you go left, you'll go the east side of Bell Rock and have excellent views of Lee Mountain and Courthouse Butte. The trail becomes very narrow with large drop offs so we recommend you turn around after about 0.1 mile {5}. But take a few minutes to enjoy the views. Then return to where you came up on Bell Rock Climb and proceed to the south and west (to the right) on the large flat area. Vortex energy has been reported all over Bell Rock so you may feel the energy. (Additional information on vortexes can be found on page 144.)

After about 0.8 mile, you'll come to a cairn and see that just beyond the cairn, there is a trail on the slickrock continuing around Bell Rock {6}. If you want to climb up to a vortex area known as the Meditation Perch, follow the slickrock around Bell Rock and you'll see the Meditation Perch ahead {7}. After you visit the vortex, return to the cairn {6} then make a left turn to descend Bell Rock. You'll see Bell Rock Pathway below so make a right turn {8} then follow Bell

Rock Pathway for 0.1 mile then make a left turn onto to the Bell Rock Trail {2} to return to the parking area {1}.

Note: You'll see several cairns above you high up on Bell Rock. To access these cairns requires steep climbs on smooth rocks. If you attempt, be extremely careful.

Color Photos: Scan the QR code for color photos of this trail

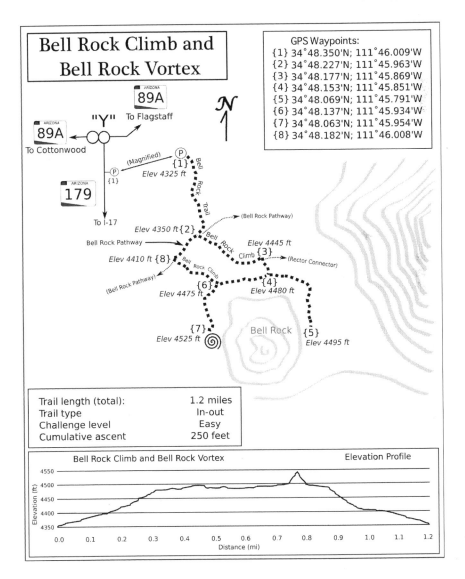

Bell Rock Climb and Bell Rock Vortex

GPS Waypoints:
{1} 34°48.350'N; 111°46.009'W
{2} 34°48.227'N; 111°45.963'W
{3} 34°48.177'N; 111°45.869'W
{4} 34°48.153'N; 111°45.851'W
{5} 34°48.069'N; 111°45.791'W
{6} 34°48.137'N; 111°45.934'W
{7} 34°48.063'N; 111°45.954'W
{8} 34°48.182'N; 111°46.008'W

Trail length (total):	1.2 miles
Trail type	In-out
Challenge level	Easy
Cumulative ascent	250 feet

Bell Rock Climb and Bell Rock Vortex — Elevation Profile

Bell Rock Loop ★

Summary: Circle Bell Rock on this pleasant easy loop

Challenge Level: Easy

Hiking Distance: About 1.9 miles round trip

Hiking Time: About about 1 hour round trip

Trail Popularity:

Trailhead Directions: From the "Y" roundabout (see page 5), drive south on SR 179 for about 5 miles to the parking area. After you drive about 3.2 miles, just past the Back O' Beyond roundabout, SR 179 becomes a divided highway. Continue driving south. About 1.8 miles beyond the Back O' Beyond roundabout, southbound SR 179 adds a passing lane on the left. From the passing lane, turn left at the sign for the Court House Vista parking area {1} (it's the second scenic view on the left side of SR 179). Before you turn, you'll see Bell Rock ahead of you on the left side of SR 179. There are toilets at the parking area. The trail starts just beyond the interpretive signboard.

Description: After you park in the Court House Vista parking area, walk past the interpretive signboard then proceed straight ahead on the Bell Rock Trail. Follow it for 0.2 mile to the intersection with the Bell Rock Pathway (BRP) Trail {2}. Continue straight ahead and make a slight left onto the Bell Rock Climb to hike the loop in a clockwise direction. In about 0.1 mile (and after climbing up about 65 feet), you'll intersect the Rector Connector Trail {3}. Make a left turn here then continue on the Rector Connector Trail. You'll come to a nice view area in about another 0.1 mile {4} then the trail makes a left turn {5}. The views from the Rector Connector Trail are very nice throughout its length. At 1 mile, you'll intersect the Courthouse Butte Loop Trail {6}. Make a right turn onto Courthouse Butte Loop then follow it for another 0.2 mile then make another right turn onto Bell Rock Pathway {7}.

Proceed on the Bell Rock Pathway for another 0.6 mile and you'll come to the western end of the Bell Rock Climb {8}. Continue on for another 0.1 mile then turn left onto the Bell Rock Trail {2} back to the parking lot {1}. If you don't mind a steep descent, hike the loop in the counterclockwise direction.

Color Photos: Scan the QR code for color photos of this trail

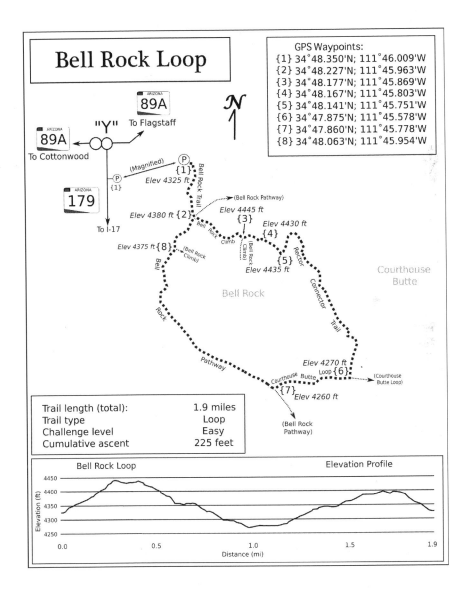

Bell Rock Loop

GPS Waypoints:
{1} 34°48.350'N; 111°46.009'W
{2} 34°48.227'N; 111°45.963'W
{3} 34°48.177'N; 111°45.869'W
{4} 34°48.167'N; 111°45.803'W
{5} 34°48.141'N; 111°45.751'W
{6} 34°47.875'N; 111°45.578'W
{7} 34°47.860'N; 111°45.778'W
{8} 34°48.063'N; 111°45.954'W

ARIZONA 89A
"Y" To Flagstaff
ARIZONA 89A
To Cottonwood
ARIZONA 179
To I-17

(Magnified)
{1}
Elev 4325 ft
Bell Rock Trail
(Bell Rock Pathway)
Elev 4445 ft
{3}
Elev 4430 ft
{4}
Elev 4380 ft {2}
Bell Rock Climb
Elev 4375 ft {8}
(Bell Rock Climb)
(Bell Rock Climb)
{5}
Elev 4435 ft
Rector
Bell Rock
Connector Trail
Courthouse Butte
Bell Rock
Pathway
Elev 4270 ft
Loop {6}
Courthouse Butte
(Courthouse Butte Loop)
{7} Elev 4260 ft
(Bell Rock Pathway)

Trail length (total):	1.9 miles
Trail type	Loop
Challenge level	Easy
Cumulative ascent	225 feet

Bell Rock Loop — **Elevation Profile**

Elevation (ft): 4250, 4300, 4350, 4400, 4450
Distance (mi): 0.0, 0.5, 1.0, 1.5, 1.9

19

Bell Rock Pathway/Templeton Loop

Summary: A loop hike with views of many of Sedona's major rock formations

Challenge Level:
Moderate

Hiking Distance:
About 4.1 miles from the Little Horse Trail parking area round trip

Hiking Time: About 2 1/2 hours round trip

Trail Popularity:

Trailhead Directions: From the "Y" roundabout (see page 5), drive south on SR 179 about 3.5 miles. You'll see a Scenic View and a hiking sign on the right side of SR 179 just past the Back O' Beyond roundabout. Turn left here then proceed across the median to the parking area {1}. There are toilets at the parking area.

Description: Go past the interpretive signboard then proceed south on the Bell Rock Pathway. You'll intersect the Little Horse trail after 0.3 mile on the left {2}. In another 0.2 mile, you'll see the HT Trail sign on the right {3}. You'll be returning on the HT Trail. As you continue on the Bell Rock Pathway, you are rewarded with excellent views of Lee Mountain, Bell Rock and Courthouse Butte.

You'll intersect the Bail Trail {4} after 1.2 miles on the left. After 1.75 miles you'll intersect the Templeton Trail on the right {5}. Turn right here onto the Templeton Trail. Follow the Templeton Trail beneath both the northbound and southbound lanes of SR 179 then you'll intersect the Easy Breezy Trail for the first time {6}. Continue on the Templeton Trail.

Look around for excellent views of Bell Rock, Courthouse Butte, Lee Mountain, Cathedral Rock and many other red rock formations. At 2.4 miles, you'll intersect the Easy Breezy Trail a second time {7}. At 2.75 miles, you'll have the best view of Cathedral Rock {8}. At 3 miles, you'll intersect the HT Trail on your right {9}. Turn right here then follow the HT Trail. You'll intersect the Easy Breezy Trail once again {10} then continue beneath both the southbound and northbound lanes of SR 179 until you intersect the Bell Rock Pathway {3} at 3.6 miles.

Make a left turn onto Bell Rock Pathway then follow it for 0.5 mile back to the parking area {1}.

Color Photos: Scan the QR code for color photos of this trail

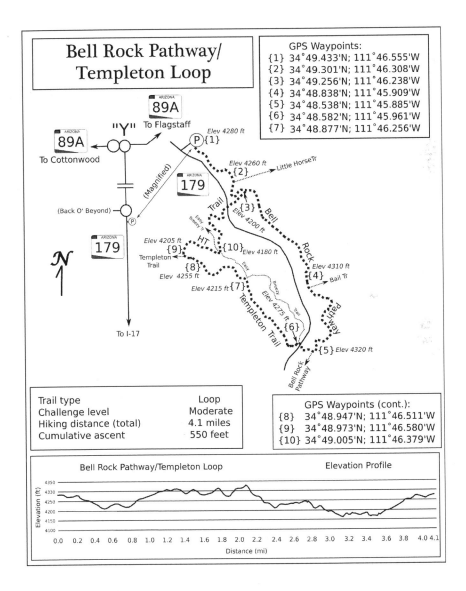

Bell Rock Pathway/ Templeton Loop		GPS Waypoints:

GPS Waypoints:
{1} 34°49.433'N; 111°46.555'W
{2} 34°49.301'N; 111°46.308'W
{3} 34°49.256'N; 111°46.238'W
{4} 34°48.838'N; 111°45.909'W
{5} 34°48.538'N; 111°45.885'W
{6} 34°48.582'N; 111°45.961'W
{7} 34°48.877'N; 111°46.256'W

Trail type	Loop
Challenge level	Moderate
Hiking distance (total)	4.1 miles
Cumulative ascent	550 feet

GPS Waypoints (cont.):
{8} 34°48.947'N; 111°46.511'W
{9} 34°48.973'N; 111°46.580'W
{10} 34°49.005'N; 111°46.379'W

Bell-Weir Trail

Summary: A sunny in-out trail that follows the path of Wet Beaver Creek with stops at a weir (a low dam) and a swimming hole

Challenge Level:
Moderate

Hiking Distance:
About 2.7 miles each way to the weir or 5.4 miles round trip; about 3.6 miles each way to the swimming hole or 7.2 miles round trip

Hiking Time: About
3 hours round trip to the weir; about 4 hours round trip to the swimming hole

Trail Popularity: 🚶🚶

Trailhead Directions: From the "Y" roundabout (see page 5), drive south on SR 179 about 14.75 miles until it intersects Interstate 17. Continue under I-17 then proceed straight on Forest Road 618 for 2 miles then turn left at the sign for the Beaver Creek Work Center. Follow the dirt road a short distance to the parking area {1}. There are toilets at the trailhead.

Description: This can be a very hot hike in the summer as there is no shade for most of the hike. To reach the Weir Trail, go through the gate at the parking area then follow the Bell Trail east along Wet Beaver Creek. About a mile from the parking area, look for a large rock on the left covered with petroglyphs placed there by Native Americans hundreds of years ago.

You will come across several trails as you hike along. The first one is the White Mesa Trail at about 1.75 miles {2}, followed by the Apache Maid Trail at 2.25 miles {3}. After 2.4 miles, you'll come to a fork {4}. Go right for 0.3 mile on the Weir Trail to reach the weir {5}. This is a good spot to take a break in the shade then return to the parking area for a 5.4 mile hike.

If you wish to visit a swimming hole known locally as The Crack, return to the fork in the trail {4} then continue to the east on the Bell Trail for about 1 mile to a sign for Bell Crossing {6}. The red rock views are very good along this part of the trail but there are places where the trail is narrow and there are large drop-offs. You'll see and hear Wet Beaver Creek on the right below.

Turn left at the sign then follow the faint trail north for 0.2 mile to The Crack {7}. At The Crack, Wet Beaver Creek is quite deep and this spot is a local favorite place for swimming.

Color Photos: Scan the QR code for color photos of this trail

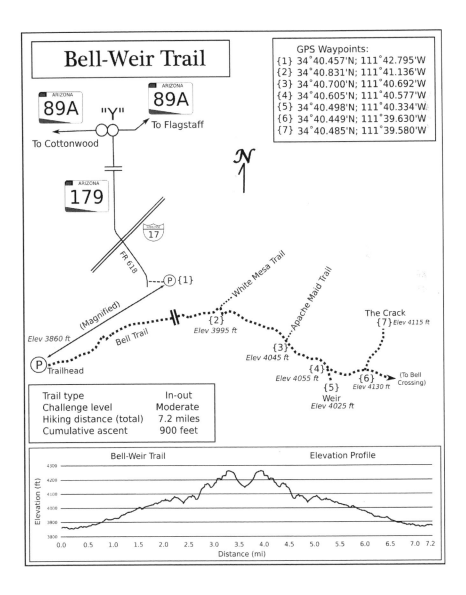

Boynton Canyon and
Boynton Vortex ★

Summary: An in-out hike to a famous Sedona vortex area then into a forested canyon with nice red rock views

Challenge Level: Easy for the vortex hike; Moderate for the canyon hike

Hiking Distance: About 1 ¼ miles round trip to the vortex; about 3.2 miles each way or 6.4 miles round trip for the canyon hike

Hiking Time: About 1 hour round trip to the vortex; about 3 hours round trip for the canyon hike

Trail Popularity:

Trailhead Directions: From the "Y" roundabout (see page 5), drive west toward Cottonwood on SR 89A about 3 miles. Turn right onto Dry Creek Road (where speed limits are strictly enforced). Stay on Dry Creek Road to a stop sign (about 3 miles) then turn left onto Boynton Pass Road. Proceed about 1.6 miles to a stop sign. Turn right, the trailhead parking is about 0.1 mile on the right {1}. There are toilets at the parking area.

Description: Boynton Canyon was named for John Boeington who was a horse rancher in the canyon around 1886. Boynton Canyon is a very popular trail. The nicest part of the trail is located beyond the Enchantment Resort. We like it for its summer shade and good red rock views. It is also a well-known vortex site. After hiking about 0.25 mile from the parking area, you'll see a sign for the Boynton Vista Trail to the right {2}. Hike the Vista Trail for about 0.4 mile slightly uphill to two tall rock formations, both of which are considered vortexes {3}. (Additional information on vortexes can be found on page 144.)

After visiting the vortexes, return to the Boynton Canyon Trail then continue to the north. The trail beside the Enchantment Resort is rocky and narrow, and is the most difficult part of the trail. Once you are past the Enchantment Resort, the trail widens and follows the canyon floor.

Just after you come to the end of the Enchantment Resort property, you can see evidence of prior habitation high up on the right {4}. Soon you'll enter a forest where the trail and views are excellent, although some of the views are blocked by the trees. You'll see some nice fall colors usually during the third week of October about 2.5 miles from the trailhead. The trail ends in a box canyon after a steep climb at the base of Secret Mountain {5}.

Color Photos: Scan the QR code for color photos of this trail

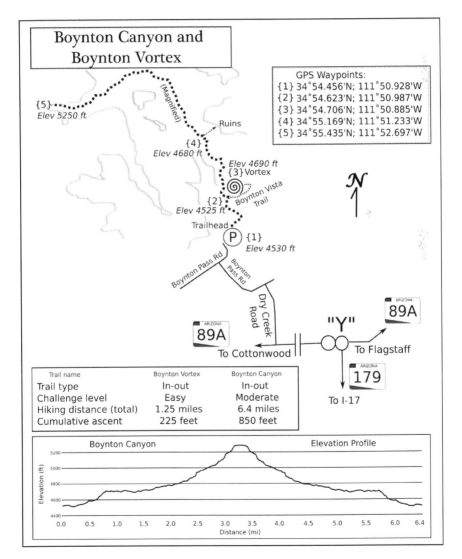

Boynton Canyon and Boynton Vortex

GPS Waypoints:
{1} 34°54.456'N; 111°50.928'W
{2} 34°54.623'N; 111°50.987'W
{3} 34°54.706'N; 111°50.885'W
{4} 34°55.169'N; 111°51.233'W
{5} 34°55.435'N; 111°52.697'W

{5}
Elev 5250 ft

(Magnified)

Ruins

{4}
Elev 4680 ft

Elev 4690 ft
{3} Vortex

Boynton Vista Trail

{2}
Elev 4525 ft

Trailhead

P {1}
Elev 4530 ft

N

Boynton Pass Rd

Boynton Pass Rd

Dry Creek Road

ARIZONA
89A

To Cottonwood

"Y"

To Flagstaff

ARIZONA
89A

ARIZONA
179

To I-17

Trail name	Boynton Vortex	Boynton Canyon
Trail type	In-out	In-out
Challenge level	Easy	Moderate
Hiking distance (total)	1.25 miles	6.4 miles
Cumulative ascent	225 feet	850 feet

Boynton Canyon   Elevation Profile

25

Brins Mesa Trail

Summary: An in-out hike to the top of a beautiful mesa with red rock views all around or a two-vehicle hike

Challenge Level:
Moderate

Hiking Distance:
This hike has two trailheads, one accessed from Jordan Road and the second off Forest Road (FR) 152. From the first trailhead, you'll hike 1.5 miles one way to the mesa top. If you hike west and down to the second trailhead, you'll hike another 2.4

miles for a total of 3.9 miles between trailheads, or if you return to the parking area, a round trip of 7.8 miles.

Hiking Time: About ¾ hour to the mesa top; about 4 hours round trip between the two trailheads

Trail Popularity: 🚶🚶

Trailhead Directions: To access the Jordan Road trailhead, from the "Y" roundabout (see page 5), drive north on SR 89A about 0.3 mile to Jordan Road. Turn left onto Jordan Road then drive to the end. Turn left onto West Park Ridge Drive then proceed through the paved cul-de-sac, continuing on the dirt road for 0.5 mile to the main parking area {1}. There are toilets at the parking area.

To access the second trailhead off FR 152, from the "Y" roundabout, drive west on SR 89A toward Cottonwood about 3 miles. Turn right onto Dry Creek Road (where speed limits are strictly enforced). Stay on Dry Creek Road for 2 miles then turn right onto FR 152. Proceed for 2.5 miles to the parking area on your right {4}.

Note: FR 152 is an extremely rough road beyond the 0.2 mile paved section; a high clearance vehicle and 4WD are strongly recommended.

Description: The trail begins on the west side of the parking area {1} and, as you begin the hike up to Brins Mesa, you are rewarded with some outstanding views. You'll be hiking up about 550 feet to reach the edge of the mesa. The trail becomes much steeper as you approach it. Once you reach the edge of the mesa {2}, you'll enjoy views all around. Look to the right for the faint trail to the Brins Mesa Overlook (see Brins Mesa Overlook Trail). Continue straight ahead to hike to the second trailhead on FR 152, which is about another 2.4 miles away. In about 1 mile, you'll intersect the Soldier Pass Trail {3}.

Hiking from the trailhead on FR 152 {4} is a pleasant, moderate uphill hike through trees. If possible, you may want to do this hike with two vehicles, one parked at each trailhead.

Color Photos: Scan the QR code for color photos of this trail

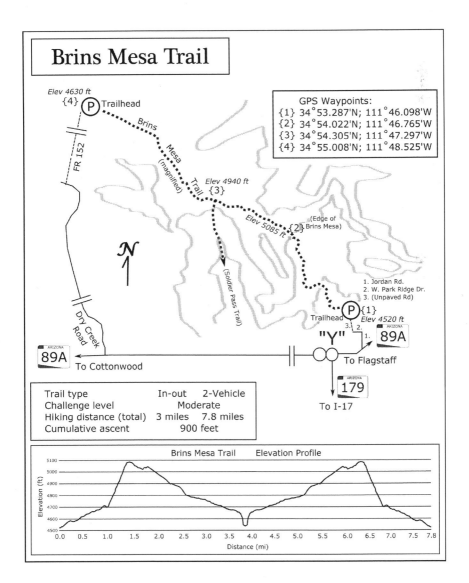

Brins Mesa Trail

Elev 4630 ft
{4} (P) Trailhead

Brins Mesa Trail (magnified)

FR 152

GPS Waypoints:
{1} 34°53.287'N; 111°46.098'W
{2} 34°54.022'N; 111°46.765'W
{3} 34°54.305'N; 111°47.297'W
{4} 34°55.008'N; 111°48.525'W

Elev 4940 ft
{3}

Elev 5085 ft
{2} (Edge of Brins Mesa)

(Soldier Pass Trail)

Dry Creek Road

ARIZONA
89A
To Cottonwood

1. Jordan Rd.
2. W. Park Ridge Dr.
3. (Unpaved Rd)

Trailhead (P) {1}
Elev 4520 ft

3. 2.
"Y"   1.   ARIZONA 89A

To Flagstaff

ARIZONA
179
To I-17

Trail type	In-out	2-Vehicle
Challenge level	Moderate	
Hiking distance (total)	3 miles	7.8 miles
Cumulative ascent	900 feet	

Brins Mesa Trail   Elevation Profile

Elevation (ft) / Distance (mi)

Brins Mesa Overlook Trail ★

Summary: A hike up to a beautiful mesa then on to a knoll with red rock views all around.

Challenge Level: Moderate

Hiking Distance: About 1.5 miles each way to the top of Brins Mesa or 3 miles round trip; add 0.7 mile one way to the overlook or 4.4 miles round trip

Hiking Time: About 2 1/2 hours round trip

Trail Popularity: 🚶🚶

Trailhead Directions: From the "Y" roundabout (see page 5), drive north on SR 89A about 0.3 mile to Jordan Road. Turn left onto Jordan Road then drive to the end. Turn left onto West Park Ridge Drive then proceed through the paved cul-de-sac, continuing on the dirt road for 0.5 mile to the main parking area {1}. There are toilets at the parking area.

Description: The trail begins on the west side of the parking area. As you begin the hike up to Brins Mesa, you are rewarded with some outstanding views. You'll be hiking up about 550 feet to reach the edge of the mesa. The trail becomes much steeper as you approach it. Immediately after you reach the mesa {2}, look for a faint trail to your right. You'll follow this trail for 0.2 mile then bear left at a fork in the trail {3}. If you go right, you'll shortly come to a scenic outcropping of red rock, which has a nice view {4}. As you continue along the left fork, the trail continues to gently rise then narrows as it follows the north side of Brins Mesa. You'll soon see the overlook ahead. A moderate amount of scrambling is needed to reach the top of the knoll, but the climb is well worth the effort. Once on top, there is a spectacular view overlooking Mormon Canyon {5}. Look high up on the rock face to the southeast. If you are lucky, that's where you may see Angel Falls flowing with the spring snow melt.

Color Photos: Scan the QR code for color photos of this trail

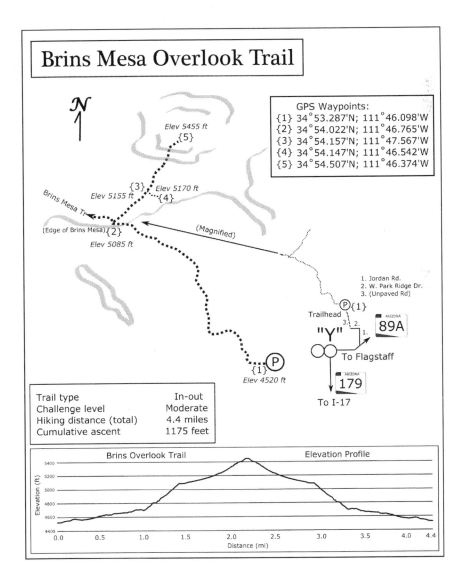

Brins Mesa Overlook Trail

GPS Waypoints:
{1} 34°53.287'N; 111°46.098'W
{2} 34°54.022'N; 111°46.765'W
{3} 34°54.157'N; 111°47.567'W
{4} 34°54.147'N; 111°46.542'W
{5} 34°54.507'N; 111°46.374'W

Elev 5455 ft
{5}

{3} Elev 5170 ft
Elev 5155 ft {4}

Brins Mesa Tr

(Edge of Brins Mesa){2} (Magnified)
Elev 5085 ft

1. Jordan Rd.
2. W. Park Ridge Dr.
3. (Unpaved Rd)

(P){1}
Trailhead
3. 2.
"Y" ARIZONA 89A

{1} (P) To Flagstaff
Elev 4520 ft

ARIZONA 179
To I-17

Trail type	In-out
Challenge level	Moderate
Hiking distance (total)	4.4 miles
Cumulative ascent	1175 feet

Brins Overlook Trail   Elevation Profile

Elevation (ft)

5400
5200
5000
4800
4600
4400

0.0   0.5   1.0   1.5   2.0   2.5   3.0   3.5   4.0 4.4
Distance (mi)

Brins Mesa/Soldier Pass Loop ★

Summary: A loop hike to the top of a beautiful mesa then down past several Sedona landmarks with red rock views all around

Challenge Level: Moderate

Hiking Distance: About 5 miles round trip

Hiking Time: About 2 ½ hours round trip

Trail Popularity:

Trailhead Directions: From the "Y" roundabout (see page 5), drive north on SR 89A about 0.3 mile to Jordan Road. Turn left onto Jordan Road then drive to the end. Turn left onto West Park Ridge Drive then proceed through the paved cul-de-sac, continuing on the dirt road for 0.5 mile to the main parking area {1}. There are toilets at the parking area.

Description: You'll actually be hiking 4 trails to complete this loop hike. The Brins Mesa Trail begins on the west side of the parking area {1}. As you begin the hike up to Brins Mesa, you are rewarded with a great view of the Cibola Mitten. At 0.6 mile, you'll have a view of Brins Mesa ahead {2}. At 1 mile, you'll cross a fairly large wash {3}then begin a rather steep ascent. Just beyond the wash there is a nice place to stop and take a rest {4}. You'll be hiking up about 550 feet to reach the edge of the mesa {5}. Once you reach the edge of the mesa {5}, you'll enjoy views all around. Continue straight ahead. The trail here is a gentle descent but is very rocky. At the 2 mile mark, you'll intersect the Soldier Pass Trail {6}.

As you begin the Soldier Pass Trail, there is a nice place to stop and take a break at the 2.3 mile mark{7}. From here, the trail descends rather steeply. At 2.5 miles look to the left for a view of the Soldier Pass Arches {8}. You'll come to a "social trail" that leads to the arches after 2.8 miles {9} but, be advised, this trail is steep with drop offs so be extremely careful if you attempt to go to the arches. At 2.9 miles, the trail makes a left turn out of a wash {10}.

At 3.6 miles, you'll come to the Seven Sacred Pools, which usually have water in them, even when it hasn't rained for some time {11}. In another 0.3 mile, you'll come to the Devil's Kitchen, a very large sink hole {12}. Continue in an easterly direction then continue onto the Jordan Trail. At 4.3 miles, you'll intersect the

30

Cibola Trail {13}. Continue on the Cibola Trail for another 0.7 mile to return to the parking area where you started.

Color Photos: Scan the QR code for color photos of this trail

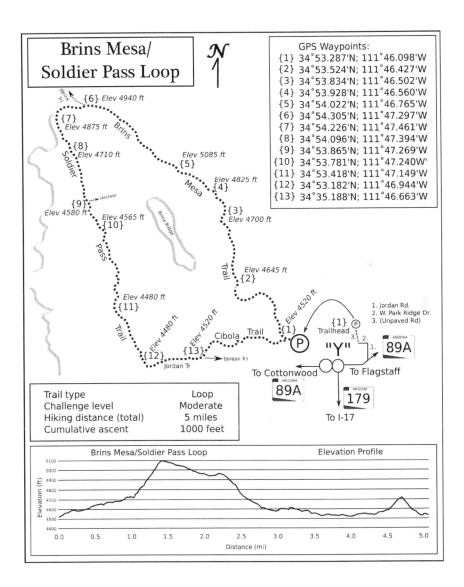

Broken Arrow/Submarine Rock Loop ★

Summary: A sunny, picturesque loop hike to the Devil's Dining Room, Submarine Rock and Chicken Point

Challenge Level: Moderate

Hiking Distance: About 1.5 miles each way to Chicken Point or 3 miles round trip; about 4 miles round trip if you hike the loop to Submarine Rock then Chicken Point and return

Hiking Time: About 2 hours round trip

Trail Popularity: 🚶🚶🚶🚶

Trailhead Directions: From the "Y" roundabout (see page 5), drive south on SR 179 for 1.5 miles to the roundabout at Morgan Road. Turn left (east) on Morgan Road then drive about 0.6 mile to the trailhead parking on your left (the last part is a dirt road) {1}. There is room for about 25 vehicles in the parking area.

Description: The trail is named for the movie, *Broken Arrow*, which was filmed in the area in 1950. From the parking area, go south across the jeep road to the trail. Initially, the trail essentially parallels the jeep road. You'll intersect the Twin Buttes Trail after 0.2 mile. After hiking about 0.4 mile, watch for a fence on the right which surrounds a large sinkhole known as the Devil's Dining Room {2}. As you continue along the trail, after about another 0.4 mile you'll come to a sign and a fork in the trail {3}. Continue on the Broken Arrow Trail for another 0.7 mile to Chicken Point or turn left to go to Submarine Rock.

Submarine rock is a very large rock formation with panoramic views all around. While you can scramble up on the north end, we prefer to hike around to the south end where it is easy to get on the top of Submarine Rock. To get to Chicken Point from the south end of Submarine Rock, look down and you'll see where the Pink Jeeps park. Go down to that parking area then follow the jeep road southwest. Be sure to stay out of the way of the jeeps as you hike along this narrow road.

Chicken Point is named for thrill-seeking jeep drivers who once dared to drive close to the edge of the point (jeep access is no longer permitted on Chicken Point). If you look to the south, you'll see a chicken-shaped rock high up on the red rock cliff. Chicken Point is a nice place for a snack break as the views are outstanding {5}. You'll likely encounter some Pink Jeeps as the Broken Arrow tour brings many visitors to this beautiful area.

Color Photos: Scan the QR code for color photos of this trail

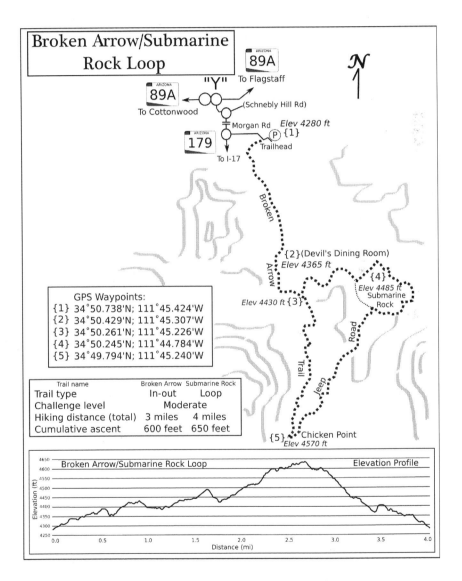

Canyon of Fools/Mescal Loop

Summary: An in-out or loop hike that provides great red rock views of Mescal Mountain

Challenge

Level: Moderate

Hiking

Distance: About a 2.6 mile in-out hike or a 3 mile loop

Hiking Time:

About 1 ½ hours round trip for the in-out hike; about 2 hours for the loop hike round trip

Trail

Popularity:

Trailhead Directions: From the "Y" roundabout (see page 5), drive west toward Cottonwood on SR 89A about 3 miles. Turn right onto Dry Creek Road (where speed limits are strictly enforced). Stay on Dry Creek Road to a stop sign (about 3 miles) then turn left onto Boynton Pass Road. Proceed about 0.6 mile to a small unmarked parking area on the right {1}. There is room for about 4 vehicles here on the north side of Boynton Pass Road and about 4 more vehicles on the south side (where the Dawa Trail begins). The trail begins on the north side of the road.

Description: We like this trail because the terrain is so different than other trails. But you must be alert for mountain bikers around several blind corners. Shortly beyond the trail marker, turn right then follow a narrow canyon with high walls for about 0.4 mile. This is the "Fools" part of the canyon. You'll note that the mountain bikers sometimes take a path parallel to the canyon but you should try to stay in the wash. As you continue north, you'll intersect the Yucca Trail after 0.5 mile and begin to have excellent views of Mescal Mountain ahead {2}. Turn left (north) here to continue on the Canyon of Fools Trail. You'll soon be in a forest of junipers and pinyon pines and come to a nice spot for a break at 1.1 miles {3}. You'll intersect the Mescal Trail after 1.3 miles {4}. Return the same way for a 2.6 mile hike.

If you want to hike a loop, turn right at {4} then follow the Mescal Trail. This part of the Mescal Trail provides wonderful up-close views of Mescal Mountain. You'll find signs indicating Difficult and Extreme portions of the trail for the mountain bikers. We recommend you hike the Difficult path. After 0.7 mile, turn right onto the Yucca Trail {5}. You have great panoramic views of Mescal Mountain for the first 0.3 mile. Follow the Yucca Trail for 0.4 mile to the intersection with the Canyon of Fools Trail {2}. Turn left (south) here then follow the Canyon of Fools Trail back to the parking area for a 3 mile hike.

Note: Stay alert for mountain bikers in front of and behind you in the "Fools" part of the canyon because it is very narrow in places and there are several blind corners. Do not hike the Canyon of Fools Trail after a hard rain as the narrow canyon may be filled with fast moving water.

Color Photos: Scan the QR code for color photos of this trail

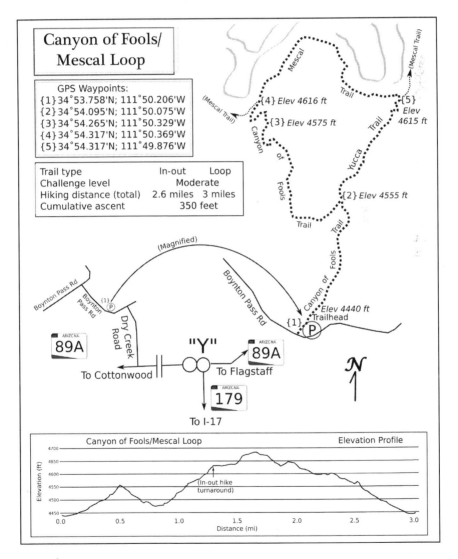

Cathedral Rock Trail and
Cathedral Vortex Trail ★

Summary: A steep, sunny in-out hike to the saddle of Cathedral Rock for spectacular views all around and the location of one of Sedona's famous vortex sites

Challenge Level: Hard

Hiking Distance: About 0.75 miles each way or 1.5 miles round trip

Hiking Time: About 1 ½ hour round trip

Trail Popularity: 🧑‍🤝‍🧑 🧑‍🤝‍🧑 🧑‍🤝‍🧑

Trailhead Directions: From the "Y" roundabout (see page 5), drive south on SR 179 about 3.2 miles to the Back O' Beyond roundabout. Turn right then go west on the Back O' Beyond Road for about 0.75 mile. The main parking area with 18 spots and the overflow parking area with 22 spots are on your left {1}. If the parking areas are full, see the Baldwin Loop Trail or HT/Easy Breezy Loop description.

Description: If you want to get up close and personal with Cathedral Rock, this short, strenuous hike is for you. The trail begins on the right (west) side of the main parking area on Back 'O Beyond Road.. You'll start out crossing a dry creek bed. Continue climbing up until the trail intersects the Templeton Trail {2}. Turn right then go about 60 paces to the branching off of the Cathedral Rock Trail on your left {3}.

From here, the trail becomes very steep. Good hiking boots or other footwear with good traction is recommended. Once you arrive at the saddle of Cathedral

Rock {4}, you are at the location of one of four main vortex sites in Sedona. (Additional information on vortexes can be found on page 144.)

There are short trails along the south side of the east and west rock formations that lead to some good views, although the footing can be tricky.

Note: If heights, an extremely steep trail or tenuous footing bothers you, or the trail is wet or snowy (making it slippery), we do not recommend this trail.

Color Photos: Scan the QR code for color photos of this trail

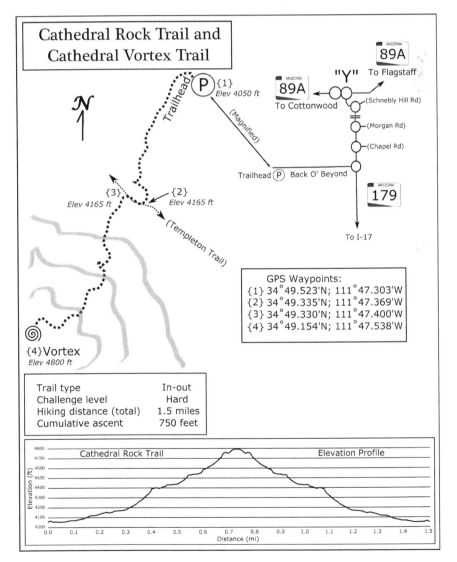

Trail type	In-out
Challenge level	Hard
Hiking distance (total)	1.5 miles
Cumulative ascent	750 feet

Chimney Rock Lower Loop

Summary: A loop hike around the base of Chimney Rock and Little Sugarloaf with panoramic views

Challenge Level: Easy

Hiking Distance: About 3 miles loop, including overlook

Hiking Time: About 2 hours round trip

Trail Popularity: 🚶🚶 🚶🚶 🚶🚶 🚶🚶

Trailhead Directions: From the "Y" roundabout (see page 5), drive west toward Cottonwood on SR 89A about 3 miles. Turn right onto Dry Creek Road (where speed limits are strictly enforced) then proceed for 0.5 mile. Turn right onto Thunder Mountain Road then drive 0.7 mile. The parking area is on your left {1}. The entrance gate opens each day at 8:00 am; the exit gate is never closed.

Description: You'll begin by hiking the Thunder Mountain Trail. From the parking area, go west past the signboard for about 100 feet then turn right onto the Thunder Mountain Trail. In 0.1 miles, you'll come to the intersection of Thunder Mountain and Chimney Rock Trails {2}. Turn right here to continue on the Thunder Mountain Trail.

As you circle Chimney Rock, you'll soon see a large water tank on the right, and intersect a "social trail" after 0.4 mile {3}. Next you'll intersect the Andante Trail{4}. After 0.7 mile, the Thunder Mountain Trail goes off to the right {5}. Turn left here onto the Chimney Pass Trail.

In 0.2 mile, look for a faint trail off to the right which leads to a scenic overlook {6}. You'll hike around the base of the first rock outcropping then scramble up on the second rock outcropping for the scenic view {7}; it's a 0.3 mile round trip scramble but worth it for the view.

About 125 feet past the trail to the overlook is another unmarked trail {8} to the left and another scramble, which leads to the base of the chimney of Chimney Rock. As you continue on, you'll intersect the Lizard Head Trail on the right {9} and an unmarked "social trail" {10} where you should bear left. At 1.4 miles, you'll intersect the Lower Chimney Rock Trail {11}. Turn right here. You'll shortly see a steep trail on the left, which leads to the summit on Little Sugarloaf. You'll have some nice views of Lizard Head Rock, Cockscomb and the 3 rock fingers of rock that make up Chimney Rock. The remainder of the trail is relatively flat. At about 2.6 miles, you pass through a fence {12}, then hike parallel with telephone poles for 0.1 mile. In another 0.25 mile you'll intersect a connector trail and be just south of the parking area. Turn left here {13} to return to your vehicle.

Note: This trail is a favorite for local residents so you'll likely encounter people walking their dogs.

Color Photos: Scan the QR code for color photos of this trail

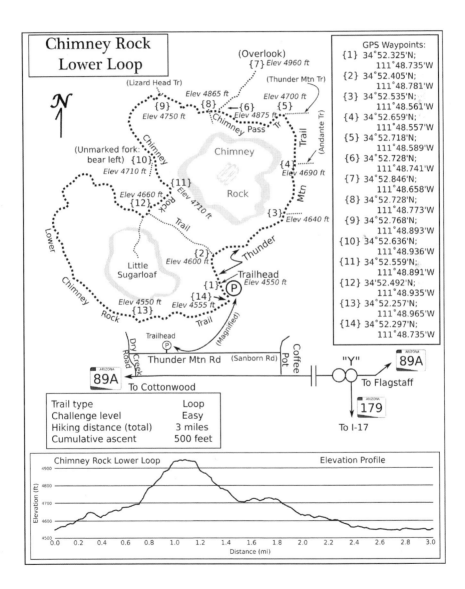

Chimney Rock Upper Loop ★

Summary: A loop hike around the base of Chimney Rock with panoramic views

Challenge Level: Easy

Hiking Distance: About a 2 mile loop, including overlook

Hiking Time: About 1 1/2 hours round trip

Trail Popularity:

Trailhead Directions:
From the "Y" roundabout (see page 5), drive west toward Cottonwood on SR 89A about 3 miles. Turn right onto Dry Creek Road (where speed limits are strictly enforced) then proceed for 0.5 mile. Turn right onto Thunder Mountain Road then drive 0.7 mile. The parking area is on your left {1}. The entrance gate opens each day at 8:00 am; the exit gate is never closed.

Description: You'll actually be hiking the Thunder Mountain and Chimney Rock Trails for this hike. From the parking area, go west past the signboard for about 100 feet then turn right onto the Thunder Mountain Trail. In 0.1 miles, you'll come to the intersection of Thunder Mountain and Chimney Rock Trails {2}.

For a morning hike, turn right here to hike in a counterclockwise direction because the views are better with the sun at your back. For an afternoon hike, continue straight ahead to hike in a clockwise direction.

As you circle Chimney Rock in the counterclockwise direction, you'll soon see a large water tank on the right, and intersect a "social trail" after 0.4 mile {3}. Next you'll intersect the Andante Trail {4}. After 0.7 mile, the Thunder Mountain Trail goes off to the right {5}. Turn left here onto the Chimney Pass Trail.

In 0.2 mile, look for a faint trail off to the right which leads to a scenic overlook {6}. You'll hike around the base of the first rock outcropping then scramble up on the second rock outcropping for the scenic view {7}; it's a 0.3 mile round trip scramble but worth it for the view.

About 125 feet past the trail to the overlook is another unmarked trail {8} to the left and another scramble, which leads to the base of the chimney of Chimney Rock. As you continue on, you'll intersect the Lizard Head Trail on the right {9} and an unmarked "social trail" {10} where you should bear left. At 1.4 miles, you'll intersect a steep trail, which leads to the summit on Little Sugarloaf {11}; stay left to complete the Chimney Rock Loop.

NOTE: The signage on the trail shows Upper Chimney Rock Trail and Lower Chimney Rock Trail at various places between {8} and {2}. Don't worry, you are on the correct trail.

Note: This trail is a favorite for local residents so you'll likely encounter people walking their dogs.

Color Photos: Scan the QR code for color photos of this trail

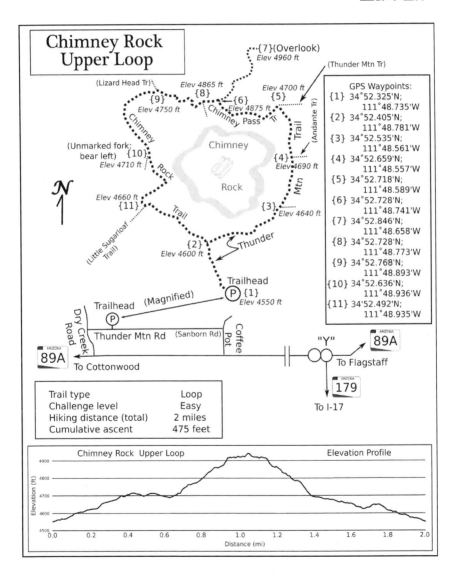

Trail type	Loop
Challenge level	Easy
Hiking distance (total)	2 miles
Cumulative ascent	475 feet

Chuckwagon In-Out Trail

Summary: A pleasant hike on a mountain bike trail that parallels Forest Road 152 with partial shade, good red rock views all around and is an alternative way to get to the Devil's Bridge Trail

Challenge Level: Moderate

Hiking Distance: About 3.8 miles each way from the Dry Creek Vista parking area or 7.6 miles round trip; about 2.8 miles each way from the Long Canyon Road parking area or 5.6 miles round trip

Hiking Time: About 4 hours round trip from the Dry Creek Vista parking area; about 3 hours round trip from the Long Canyon Road parking area

Trail Popularity: 🚶🚶🚶

Trailhead Directions: There are two primary ways to access this trail. From the "Y" roundabout (see page 5), drive west toward Cottonwood on SR 89A about 3 miles. Turn right onto Dry Creek Road (where speed limits are strictly enforced). Stay on Dry Creek Road for about 2 miles then turn right onto Forest Road (FR) 152. Drive 0.2 mile on the paved FR 152 to the Dry Creek Vista parking area on the left {1}. Or, continue on Dry Creek Road for an additional 1 mile then turn right onto Long Canyon Road. Drive 0.3 mile to the parking area on the right (also used for the Mescal Trail) {3}. There are toilets and picnic tables at the Dry Creek Vista parking area {1}.

Description: From the Dry Creek Vista parking area {1}, the Chuckwagon Trail begins on the right of the interpretive signboard. After 0.7 mile, you'll come to a fork in the trail and a signpost{2}. The right fork leads to FR 152 and is a shortcut to Devil's Bridge (although you'll be hiking on dusty FR 152 road). Stay left to continue on the Chuckwagon Trail. In 1.1 miles, you'll intersect the connector trail from the Long Canyon parking area {5} on the left. If you begin at the Long Canyon parking area {3}, look for a sign that points south to the Chuckwagon Trail at the northeast end of the parking area. Hike this connector trail south 0.25 mile to the intersection with the Chuckwagon Trail {5} then turn left. You'll have some very nice panoramic views to the north {6}.

Hike northeast for 0.8 mile from {5} to a sign To Devils Bridge {7} which will lead you to Devil's Bridge {4} (see the Devil's Bridge Trail). There is a nice spot for a snack 0.15 mile past the turn to Devil's Bridge {8}. As you continue, you'll have views on both sides. After about 2 additional miles, you'll come to a fork in the trail {9}. We suggest you turn around here. The right fork leads to Brins Mesa trailhead after 0.5 mile. If you'd like to hike a loop see Chuckwagon Loop.

Color Photos: Scan the QR code for color photos of this trail

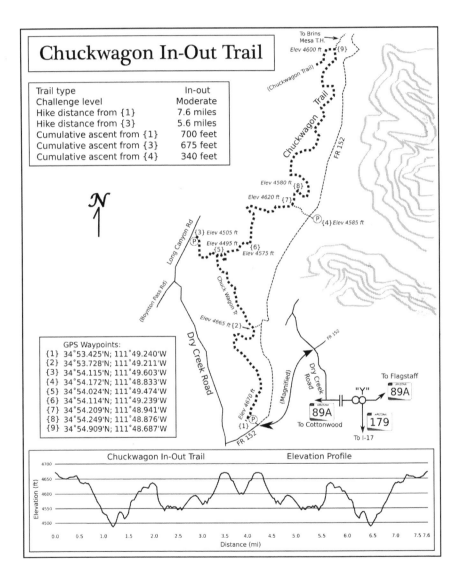

Chuckwagon Loop

Summary: A pleasant loop hike on a mountain bike trail that parallels Forest Road 152 then goes to Long Canyon Road with partial shade, good red rock views all around and is an alternative way to get to the Devil's Bridge Trail

Challenge Level:
Moderate

Hiking Distance:
About 4.7 mile loop from the Long Canyon Road parking area

Hiking Time: About 3 hours round trip from the Long Canyon Road parking area

Trail Popularity:

Trailhead Directions: From the "Y" roundabout (see page 5), drive west toward Cottonwood on SR 89A about 3 miles. Turn right onto Dry Creek Road (where speed limits are strictly enforced). Stay on Dry Creek Road for about 3 miles then turn right onto Long Canyon Road. Drive 0.3 mile to the parking area on the right (also used for the Mescal Trail) {1}.

Description: We suggest hiking this loop from the Long Canyon parking area {1}. Look for a sign that points south to the Chuckwagon Trail at the northeast end of the Long Canyon Road parking area {1}. Hike this connector trail south 0.25 mile to the intersection with the Chuckwagon Trail {2} then turn left. You'll soon have some very nice panoramic views to the north {3}.

Hike northeast for 0.8 mile from {3} to a sign To Devils Bridge {4} which will lead you to the Devil's Bridge parking area {5} (see the Devil's Bridge Trail). There is a nice spot for a snack 0.15 mile past the turn to Devil's Bridge {6}. As you continue, you'll have views on both sides. The trail continues with a series of ups and downs, but nothing too steep. After about 2 additional miles, you'll come to a fork in the trail {7}. The right fork leads to Brins Mesa trailhead after 0.5 mile. The Chuckwagon Trail continues to the left.

You'll cross a shallow wash then a deeper wash after 0.2 mile {8}. There is a nice spot to stop after another 0.6 mile {9}. The trail takes two sharp turns then is relatively flat for the next 0.6 mile until you come to Long Canyon Road {10}. Cross the road and continue just past the interpretive signboard then turn left onto the connector trail. Follow the connector trail to the intersection with the Mescal Trail {11} Turn left here then follow the Mescal Trail back to the parking area {1}.

Note: You'll likely encounter mountain bikers as this is a favorite bike trail.

Color Photos: Scan the QR code for color photos of this trail

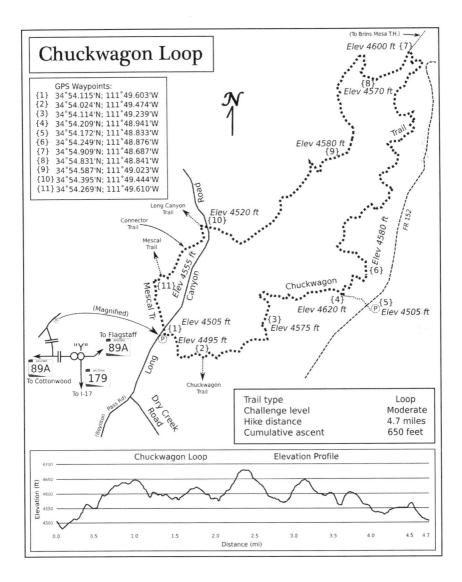

Chuckwagon Loop

GPS Waypoints:
{1} 34°54.115'N; 111°49.603'W
{2} 34°54.024'N; 111°49.474'W
{3} 34°54.114'N; 111°49.239'W
{4} 34°54.209'N; 111°48.941'W
{5} 34°54.172'N; 111°48.833'W
{6} 34°54.249'N; 111°48.876'W
{7} 34°54.909'N; 111°48.687'W
{8} 34°54.831'N; 111°48.841'W
{9} 34°54.587'N; 111°49.023'W
{10} 34°54.395'N; 111°49.444'W
{11} 34°54.269'N; 111°49.610'W

(To Brins Mesa T.H.) →
Elev 4600 ft {7}
{8}
Elev 4570 ft
Elev 4580 ft
{9}
Trail
FR 152
Elev 4580 ft
{6}
Long Canyon Trail
Elev 4520 ft
{10}
Connector Trail
Mescal Trail
Road
Canyon
Chuckwagon
{4}
Elev 4620 ft
{5}
Elev 4505 ft
{11}
Elev 4555 ft
Mescal Tr
(Magnified)
To Flagstaff
89A
Elev 4505 ft
{3}
Elev 4575 ft
{1}
Elev 4495 ft
{2}
"Y"
89A
To Cottonwood
179
To I-17
(Boynton Pass Rd)
Long
Canyon
Dry Creek Road
Chuckwagon Trail

Trail type	Loop
Challenge level	Moderate
Hike distance	4.7 miles
Cumulative ascent	650 feet

Chuckwagon Loop   Elevation Profile

Elevation (ft)
4700
4650
4600
4550
4500

0.0   0.5   1.0   1.5   2.0   2.5   3.0   3.5   4.0   4.5 4.7
Distance (mi)

Cibola Pass/Jordan Loop

Summary: This close-to-town, in-out hike provides some spectacular red rock views with the option to hike a loop, visit the Devil's Kitchen sinkhole and the Seven Sacred Pools

Challenge Level:
Moderate

Hiking Distance:
About 0.75 mile each way or 1.5 miles round trip; about a 2 mile loop if you hike the Cibola Pass Trail then return on the Jordan Trail; about 3.6 miles loop if you hike the Cibola Pass Trail to the Jordan Trail to the Soldier Pass Trail to

the Seven Sacred Pools returning via the Jordan Trail

Hiking Time: About 1 ½ hour round trip for the Cibola/Jordan loop; about 2 ½ hours round trip to the Seven Sacred Pools and return

Trail Popularity: 🚶🚶 🚶🚶 🚶🚶

Trailhead Directions: From the "Y" roundabout (see page 5), drive north on SR 89A about 0.3 mile to Jordan Road. Turn left onto Jordan Road then drive to the end. Turn left onto West Park Ridge Drive then proceed through the paved cul-de-sac, continuing on the dirt road for 0.5 mile to the main parking area {1}. There are toilets at the parking area.

Description: Begin hiking the trail on the west side of the parking area near the toilets. Go through the opening in the cable fence. The Cibola Pass Trail branches left from the Brins Mesa Trail after about 400 feet {2}. The trail is quite steep in places. As you proceed, you'll have some very nice red rock views including the Cibola Mitten rock formation. At about 0.4 mile, you'll approach two fence posts on the left side {3}. If you go straight for a short distance, you'll have some great views. Return to the fence posts then continue on the trail. You'll intersect the Jordan Trail after hiking 0.75 mile {4}. Turn around here to return to the parking area via the Cibola Trail, or turn south and follow the Jordan Trail back to the parking area for a 2 mile loop.

Or proceed west on the Jordan Trail for 0.4 mile to the Soldier Pass Trail. Turn right onto the Soldier Pass Trail, which leads to Devil's Kitchen (a very large sink hole) {5}. Continue on the Soldier Pass Trail for 0.4 mile and you'll arrive at the Seven Sacred Pools {6}. You'll have hiked about 3.6 miles for the entire

46

hike from the Seven Sacred Pools when you return to the parking area via the Jordan Trail.

Color Photos: Scan the QR code for color photos of this trail

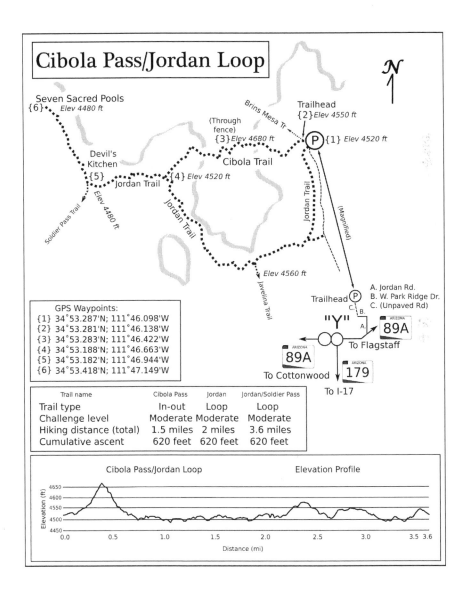

Cibola Pass/Jordan Loop

GPS Waypoints:
{1} 34°53.287'N; 111°46.098'W
{2} 34°53.281'N; 111°46.138'W
{3} 34°53.283'N; 111°46.422'W
{4} 34°53.188'N; 111°46.663'W
{5} 34°53.182'N; 111°46.944'W
{6} 34°53.418'N; 111°47.149'W

Trail name	Cibola Pass	Jordan	Jordan/Soldier Pass
Trail type	In-out	Loop	Loop
Challenge level	Moderate	Moderate	Moderate
Hiking distance (total)	1.5 miles	2 miles	3.6 miles
Cumulative ascent	620 feet	620 feet	620 feet

Cibola Pass/Jordan Loop — Elevation Profile

Cockscomb/Aerie Loop

Summary: A loop hike circling Doe Mountain with excellent views of Doe Mountain, Bear Mountain, Fay Canyon and Boynton Canyon

Challenge Level: Moderate

Hiking Distance: 5.4 miles around Doe Mountain using the Cockscomb and Aerie Trails to make a loop hike

Hiking Time: About 3 hours round trip

Trail Popularity: 👫

Trailhead Directions: From the "Y" roundabout (see page 5), drive west toward Cottonwood on SR 89A about 3 miles. Turn right onto Dry Creek Road (where speed limits are strictly enforced). Stay on Dry Creek Road to a stop sign (about 3 miles) then turn left onto Boynton Pass Road. Proceed about 1.6 miles to a stop sign. Turn left then continue on Boynton Pass Road. Drive about 2.5 miles then turn left onto Aerie Road, which is about 0.5 mile past the Doe Mountain/Bear Mountain parking area on the left side of Boynton Pass Road. Follow Aerie Road then take the right fork to the parking area {1}.

Description: You'll first be hiking the Cockscomb Trail and return via the Aerie Trail to complete the loop. The trail begins near the signboard at the west end of the parking lot. About 100 feet south of the parking area is a trail sign. Go straight then follow the Cockscomb Trail to hike a counter clockwise loop around the south, east then north side of Doe Mountain. The best views are along the north side of Doe Mountain on the Aerie Trail.

Follow the Cockscomb Trail until you come to a fence after 0.9 mile where you'll see a "social trail" on the right after 1.1 miles. Turn left here. You'll cross a road after 1.2 miles then intersect the Rupp Trail after 1.6 miles {2}.

You'll intersect the Dawa Trail after 2.6 miles {3} and the Aerie Trail after another 0.8 mile {4}. If you continue straight on the Cockscomb Trail, you'll come to the Fay Canyon parking area. Turn left (west) to follow the Aerie Trail across the north side of Doe Mountain to complete the loop.

At 4.6 miles you'll cross the trail leading up to Doe Mountain {5}. The Aerie Trail takes a slight jog here at the intersection with the Doe Mountain Trail but it is well-marked. Continue on the Aerie Trail back to the parking area {1} on your 5.4 mile hike.

Color Photos: Scan the QR code for color photos of this trail

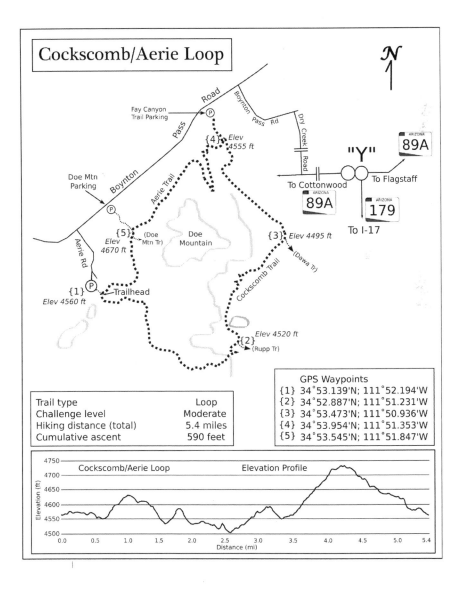

Trail type	Loop
Challenge level	Moderate
Hiking distance (total)	5.4 miles
Cumulative ascent	590 feet

GPS Waypoints
{1} 34°53.139'N; 111°52.194'W
{2} 34°52.887'N; 111°51.231'W
{3} 34°53.473'N; 111°50.936'W
{4} 34°53.954'N; 111°51.353'W
{5} 34°53.545'N; 111°51.847'W

Coffeepot Trail

Summary: An in-town, in-out hike that takes you to the base of Coffeepot Rock

Challenge Level: Easy

Hiking Distance: About 1.2 miles each way or 2.4 miles round trip

Hiking Time: About 1 ½ hours round trip

Trail Popularity: 🚶🚶🚶

Trailhead Directions: From the "Y" roundabout (see page 5), drive west toward Cottonwood on SR 89A for just under 2 miles then turn right onto Coffeepot Drive. Drive about 0.5 miles then turn left at the stop sign onto Sanborn. Continue to the second street then turn right onto Little Elf. Little Elf ends at Buena Vista so make a short right onto Buena Vista then a quick left into the parking area {1}. This parking area also serves the Teacup, Thunder Mountain and Sugarloaf Trails. It has only 10 spots so can fill quickly.

Description: About 50 feet past the interpretive signboard near the parking area, look for a sign on the right {2}. Follow the Sugarloaf-Teacup Trail for 0.3 mile. Turn right at the next sign {3} then continue on the Teacup Trail. You'll soon come to a sign for the Sugarloaf Summit Loop Trail {4}. Continue on the Teacup Trail for another 0.15 mile then turn left {5} onto an unmarked trail that we call the Coffeepot Trail, which will lead you to the base of Coffeepot Rock. There are many "social trails" in this area so be sure to follow the cairns until you turn onto the Coffeepot Trail. There aren't any cairns along this trail, but it is

50

easy to follow. You'll hike on rock ledges under Coffeepot Rock until you come to Shark Rock {6}, which looks like the open mouth of a giant shark. Continue on until the ledges eventually become too narrow and steep to go any farther {7}. Return the way you came for a 2.4 mile hike.

There is little shade on this trail making this a hot summer hike.

Color Photos: Scan the QR code for color photos of this trail

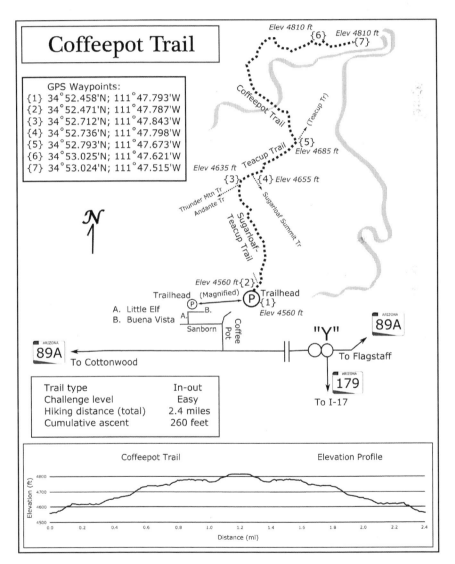

Coffeepot Trail

GPS Waypoints:
{1} 34°52.458'N; 111°47.793'W
{2} 34°52.471'N; 111°47.787'W
{3} 34°52.712'N; 111°47.843'W
{4} 34°52.736'N; 111°47.798'W
{5} 34°52.793'N; 111°47.673'W
{6} 34°53.025'N; 111°47.621'W
{7} 34°53.024'N; 111°47.515'W

Elev 4810 ft {6}   Elev 4810 ft {7}

Coffeepot Trail

(Teacup Tr)

Teacup Trail {5} Elev 4685 ft

Elev 4635 ft {3} {4} Elev 4655 ft

Thunder Mtn Tr
Andante Tr

Sugarloaf Summit Tr

Sugarloaf-Teacup Trail

𝒩
↑

Elev 4560 ft {2}
Trailhead (Magnified)   P Trailhead {1}
A. Little Elf   A. Elev 4560 ft
B. Buena Vista   B.
Sanborn   Coffee Pot

"Y"

ARIZONA 89A

ARIZONA 89A
To Cottonwood

To Flagstaff

ARIZONA 179
To I-17

Trail type	In-out
Challenge level	Easy
Hiking distance (total)	2.4 miles
Cumulative ascent	260 feet

Coffeepot Trail   Elevation Profile

Elevation (ft)

4800
4700
4600
4500
0.0 0.2 0.4 0.6 0.8 1.0 1.2 1.4 1.6 1.8 2.0 2.2 2.4
Distance (mi)

Cookstove to Harding Springs Trails

Summary: A two-vehicle hike up the side of Oak Creek Canyon through a pine forest and down again

Challenge Level: Hard

Hiking Distance: About 2.9 miles

Hiking Time: About 3 hours roundtrip

Trail Popularity: 🏃

Trailhead Directions: This is a two-vehicle hike. Park one vehicle at Cave Springs and one at the artesian well at Pine Flats. From the "Y" roundabout (see page 5), drive north on SR 89A about 11.7 miles (mile marker 385.6) then turn left toward the Cave Springs campground. Park your first vehicle in the parking area on the right {13}. Continue north on SR 89A about 1.3 miles (mile marker 386.9) to the Pine Flats campground. Park the other vehicle on the west side of SR 89A near the well {1}, but don't block access to the well.

Description: Once you park the second vehicle, cross SR 89A to the sign for the Cookstove Trail, which is directly across from the well then hike up the east side of Oak Creek Canyon. The trail is very steep and there are places where erosion has taken place making footing tricky. You'll be climbing about 750 feet to a flat mesa {2}. Turn right then hike south following the edge of Oak Creek Canyon. You'll turn away from Oak Creek Canyon to skirt a side canyon then make a series of turns {3}{4}{5}. You'll cross several washes and hike along an old road then rejoin the trail and intersect the Harding Springs Trail {6}{7}{8} {9}{10}. Before starting down the steep Harding Springs Trail (to your other vehicle), continue about 450 feet south along the canyon rim to a nice overlook area {11}. The unmarked, unmaintained trail is difficult to follow at times, and is not a straight line between the top of the Cookstove Trail and the Harding

Springs Trail. Also, you'll be climbing over some fallen trees. We strongly recommend using a portable GPS unit to hike between the trails across the mesa (See https://greatsedonahikes.com/gps/gps.html). This is a shady hike in the summer, with good foliage colors in the fall. Because of potential slippery conditions, do not attempt this hike if the trail is wet or snow-covered.

Color Photos: Scan the QR code for color photos of this trail

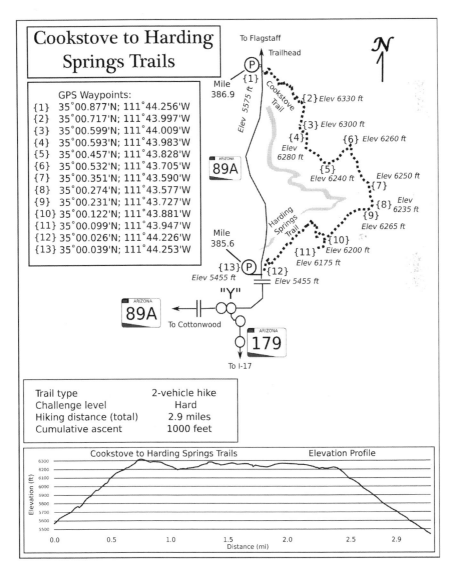

GPS Waypoints:	
{1}	35°00.877'N; 111°44.256'W
{2}	35°00.717'N; 111°43.997'W
{3}	35°00.599'N; 111°44.009'W
{4}	35°00.593'N; 111°43.983'W
{5}	35°00.457'N; 111°43.828'W
{6}	35°00.532'N; 111°43.705'W
{7}	35°00.351'N; 111°43.590'W
{8}	35°00.274'N; 111°43.577'W
{9}	35°00.231'N; 111°43.727'W
{10}	35°00.122'N; 111°43.881'W
{11}	35°00.099'N; 111°43.947'W
{12}	35°00.026'N; 111°44.226'W
{13}	35°00.039'N; 111°44.253'W

Cookstove to Harding Springs Trails

Trail type	2-vehicle hike
Challenge level	Hard
Hiking distance (total)	2.9 miles
Cumulative ascent	1000 feet

53

Courthouse Butte Loop

Summary: A pleasant loop hike circling Bell Rock and Courthouse Butte near the Village of Oak Creek

Challenge Level:
Moderate

Hiking Distance:
About 4.2 miles loop

Hiking Time: About
2 ½ hours round trip

Trail Popularity:

Trailhead

Directions: There are two parking areas you can use for this hike. From the "Y" roundabout (see page 5), drive south on SR 179 for about 5 miles to the first parking area. After you drive about 3.2 miles, just past the Back O' Beyond roundabout, SR 179 becomes a divided highway. Continue driving south. About 1.8 miles beyond the Back O' Beyond roundabout, southbound SR 179 adds a passing lane on the left. From the passing lane, turn left at the sign for the Court House Vista parking area {1} (it's the second scenic view on the left side of SR 179).

Before you turn, you'll see Bell Rock ahead of you on the left side of SR 179. The trail starts on the southeast side of the parking area. After you park, walk past the interpretive signboard then proceed straight ahead on the Bell Rock Trail. Follow it for 0.1 mile to the intersection with the Courthouse Butte Loop Trail {2}.

If you continue driving south on SR 179, in 1 mile you'll come to the Bell Rock Vista, the second parking area, on your left. Turn left into the parking area {8}. There are toilets at both the parking areas. Follow the Bell Rock Pathway Trail north for about 0.5 mile until you intersect the Courthouse Butte Loop Trail {7}.

Description: This trail circling Courthouse Butte and Bell Rock combines panoramic and close-up views of these two famous rock formations as well as distant views of Rabbit Ears, the Chapel of the Holy Cross and Cathedral Rock. The trail is fairly open, so it provides limited shade making it a hot summer hike.

We like to hike this loop in the clockwise direction from the Bell Rock Vista parking area, although either direction provides great views. From the Bell Rock Vista parking area, the trail starts out wide and is defined by fences on both sides. You'll intersect several trails as you hike including the Llama Trail {3} and Big Park Loop Trail {5}{6}. A good stopping point for a snack break is near Muffin Rock, which some call UFO Rock {4}. The Courthouse Butte Loop Trail and the Big Park Loop Trail are combined between {5} and {6}. For a shortcut back to the parking lot, turn left at {6} where you'll see a sign pointing to the Big Park Loop Trail.

Color Photos: Scan the QR code for color photos of this trail

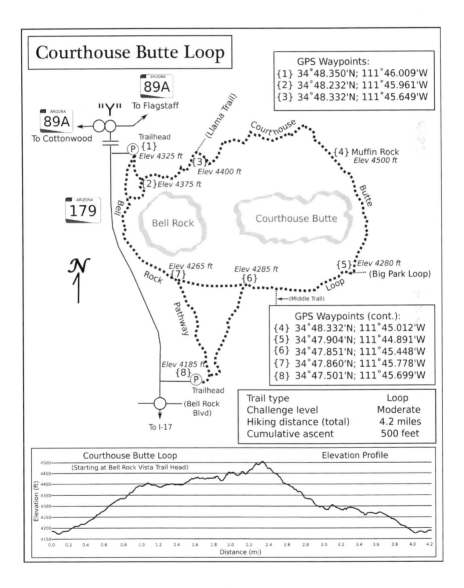

Courthouse Butte Short Loop

Summary: A pleasant loop hike circling Courthouse Butte near the Village of Oak Creek

Challenge Level: Moderate

Hiking Distance: About 4 miles loop

Hiking Time: About 2 ½ hours round trip

Trail Popularity: 🚶🚶 🚶🚶 🚶🚶

Trailhead Directions: From the "Y" roundabout (see page 5), drive south on SR 179 for about 6 miles. After you drive about 3.2 miles, just past the Back O' Beyond roundabout, SR 179 becomes a divided highway. Continue driving south. About 1.8 miles beyond the Back O' Beyond roundabout, southbound SR 179 adds a passing lane on the left. Continue past the Court House Vista parking area for another mile and turn left into the Bell Rock Vista parking area {1}. There are toilets at the parking area.

Description: This trail is similar to the Courthouse Butte Loop Trail except you'll be hiking a connector trail between Bell Rock and Courthouse Butte. It combines panoramic and close-up views of these two famous rock formations as well as distant views of Rabbit Ears, the Chapel of the Holy Cross and Cathedral Rock. The trail is fairly open, so it provides limited shade making it a hot summer hike.

We like to hike this loop in the clockwise direction. From the Bell Rock Vista parking area, hike past the interpretive signboard then follow the well defined trail. The trail starts out wide and is defined by fences on both sides. You'll soon see a sign Bell Rock Path↑ then intersect a trail and sign, Big Park Loop →. Turn right here then follow this trail a short distance then turn left at the trail and sign, To Courthouse Butte Loop. Follow this trail for 0.4 mile to the intersection with the Courthouse Butte Loop Trail {2}. Here, turn left then follow the Courthouse Butte Loop Trail for 0.1 mile to the Rector Connector Trail {3}.

Turn right then follow the Rector Connector for 0.6 mile where you'll intersect the Bell Rock Climb Trail {4}. Turn right and carefully descend the Bell Rock Climb Trail. You'll soon intersect the Bell Rock Pathway.{5}. Make a right turn onto the Bell Rock Pathway then follow the signs to the Courthouse Butte Loop Trail. After 0.2 mile, you'll intersect the Courthouse Butte Loop Trail then after another 0.2 mile the Llama Trail {6}. Continue on the Courthouse Butte Loop Trail. A good stopping point for a snack break is near Muffin Rock {7}, which some call UFO Rock.

The Courthouse Butte Loop Trail is joined by the Big Park Loop Trail {8} then you'll intersect the Middle Trail {9} then 0.25 mile later a sign pointing to the Big Park Loop Trail {2}. Turn left at {2} then follow the trail back to the parking lot {1}.

Color Photos: Scan the QR code for color photos of this trail

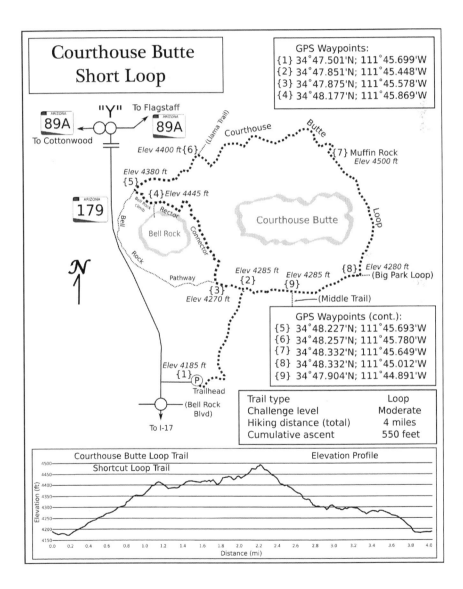

Cow Pies Trail

Summary: An in-out stroll over slickrock with nice views all around

Challenge Level: Easy

Hiking Distance: About 1 mile each way or 2 miles round trip

Hiking Time: About 1 ½ hour round trip

Trail Popularity: 🚶🚶

Trailhead Directions: From the "Y" roundabout (see page 5), drive south on SR 179 about 0.3 mile to the Schnebly Hill Roundabout then drive 270 degrees (3/4 of the way) around to Schnebly Hill Road. Proceed 3.7 miles on Schnebly Hill Road. The trailhead parking is on your right {1}. Schnebly Hill Road is paved for the first mile but the last 2.7 miles is an unpaved road and can be very rough; a high clearance vehicle and 4WD are strongly recommended.

Description: The Cow Pies area is likely named because the four huge circular sandstone mounds resemble very large cow droppings. The trailhead is across the road from the parking area. Soon you'll pass by an area dotted with small black rocks, which are pieces of lava. Some believe this to be another powerful vortex area {2}. (Additional information on vortexes can be found on page 144.) Continue along the trail for 0.3 mile then make a left turn {3} when you arrive at a large area of flat rock (known as slickrock) to go to the cow pies. If you go straight, you'll be hiking the Hangover Trail (see Hangover/Munds Wagon Loop).

As you continue to the left, you'll hike up on the cow pies, which border Bear Wallow. You'll have to do a bit of scrambling in some areas to ascend the cow pies. There isn't a defined trail so you'll be free to explore the cow pies. There are a number of areas that provide good views {4} {5}. Because the red rocks can be very slippery when wet, do not attempt this hike if the rocks are wet or there is snow or ice present.

Color Photos: Scan the QR code for color photos of this trail

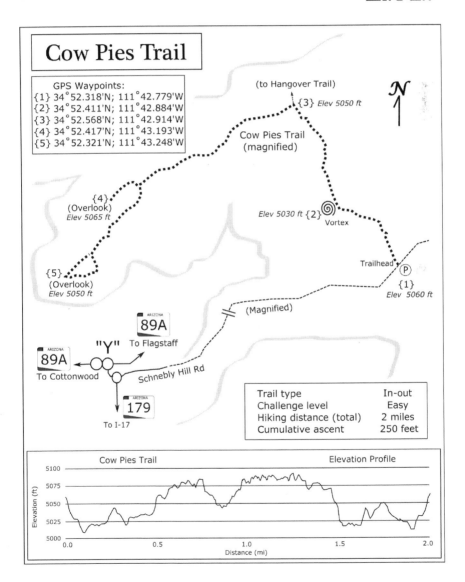

Cow Pies Trail

GPS Waypoints:
{1} 34°52.318'N; 111°42.779'W
{2} 34°52.411'N; 111°42.884'W
{3} 34°52.568'N; 111°42.914'W
{4} 34°52.417'N; 111°43.193'W
{5} 34°52.321'N; 111°43.248'W

(to Hangover Trail)

{3} Elev 5050 ft

Cow Pies Trail (magnified)

{4} (Overlook) Elev 5065 ft

Elev 5030 ft {2}
Vortex

{5} (Overlook) Elev 5050 ft

Trailhead
{1}
Elev 5060 ft

(Magnified)

ARIZONA **89A**

"Y" To Flagstaff

ARIZONA **89A**
To Cottonwood

Schnebly Hill Rd

ARIZONA **179**
To I-17

Trail type	In-out
Challenge level	Easy
Hiking distance (total)	2 miles
Cumulative ascent	250 feet

Cow Pies Trail — Elevation Profile

(Elevation profile: Elevation (ft) from 5000 to 5100 vs Distance (mi) from 0.0 to 2.0)

Devil's Bridge Trail ★

Summary: A moderate in-out climb with steep stairs up to the largest natural stone arch in the Sedona area

Challenge Level: Moderate

Hiking Distance: About 1 mile each way From the Devil's Bridge (DB) parking area or 2 miles round trip; about 2.2 miles each way from the Mescal Trail parking area or 4.4 miles round trip; about 3.1 miles each way from the Dry Creek Vista parking area or 6.2 miles round trip

Hiking Time: About 1½ hour round trip from the DB parking area; about 2 ½ hours round trip from the Mescal Trail parking area; about 3 ½ hours round trip from the Dry Creek Vista parking area

Trail Popularity: 🚶🚶 🚶🚶 🚶🚶 🚶

Trailhead Directions: From the "Y" roundabout (see page 5), drive west toward Cottonwood on SR 89A about 3 miles. Turn right onto Dry Creek Road (where speed limits are strictly enforced). Stay on Dry Creek Road for about 2 miles then turn right onto Forest Road (FR) 152. Drive for 0.2 mile and park at the Dry Creek Vista parking area {1}. If you have a high clearance vehicle, proceed for another 1.1 miles on the unpaved, very rough FR 152 to the DB parking area on your right {2}. Or rather than turn onto FR 152, a third alternative is to continue on Dry Creek Road another 1 mile then turn right onto Long Canyon Road. Drive 0.3 mile to the Mescal Trail parking area on the right {3}.

Note: FR 152 is an extremely rough road beyond the 0.2 mile paved section; a high clearance vehicle and 4WD are strongly recommended.

Description: From the Dry Creek Vista parking area {1}, go to the signboard where you'll see a small sign pointing to the right for the Chuckwagon (CW) Trail. After 0.7 mile, you'll come to a fork in the trail and a signpost {4}. The right fork leads to FR 152 and is a shortcut to Devil's Bridge (although you'll be hiking on the dusty FR 152 road). We recommend that you continue on the CW Trail. You'll pass the intersection of the trail to the Mescal Trail parking area {3} after 1.1 miles {5}. Continue on the CW Trail for a total of 2.1 miles then turn right onto the connector trail to the DB parking area across FR 152 {6}.

For most folks, we recommend starting from the Mescal Trail parking area {3}. Hike the connector trail from the northeast end of the parking area for 0.2 mile then turn left onto the CW Trail {5}. Hike for 0.8 mile to the turn to DB {6}.

Devil's Bridge is a large natural stone arch that you can walk on. It is reachable with a moderate amount of climbing (up some 400 feet); the view of the arch and from the arch are well worth the climb. The trail splits about 0.75 mile from the start, 15 feet past where you'll come to a large rock next to the trail {7}. Go straight then right to reach the top of the arch; take the left fork to go beneath the arch. If you take the trail to the top of the arch {8}, you'll be hiking up some steep natural stone steps (with no hand rails) so watch your footing. If you have a fear of heights, you may want to be extra careful on this hike, or only take the left trail to view the arch from beneath

Color Photos: Scan the QR code for color photos of this trail

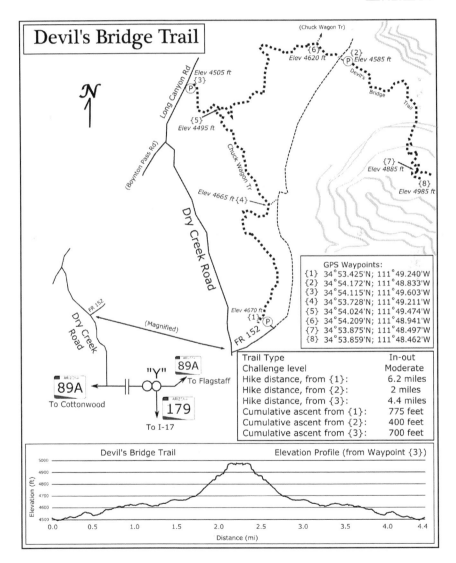

Devil's Bridge Trail

(Chuck Wagon Tr)

{6} Elev 4620 ft   {2} Elev 4585 ft

Devil's Bridge Trail

Long Canyon Rd

Elev 4505 ft {3}

{5} Elev 4495 ft

(Boynton Pass Rd)

Chuck Wagon Tr

Elev 4665 ft {4}

{7} Elev 4885 ft

{8} Elev 4985 ft

Dry Creek Road

FR 152

Dry Creek Road

(Magnified)

Elev 4670 ft {1}

FR 152

To Cottonwood

"Y"   89A

89A   To Flagstaff

179

To I-17

GPS Waypoints:
{1} 34°53.425'N; 111°49.240'W
{2} 34°54.172'N; 111°48.833'W
{3} 34°54.115'N; 111°49.603'W
{4} 34°53.728'N; 111°49.211'W
{5} 34°54.024'N; 111°49.474'W
{6} 34°54.209'N; 111°48.941'W
{7} 34°53.875'N; 111°48.497'W
{8} 34°53.859'N; 111°48.462'W

Trail Type	In-out
Challenge level	Moderate
Hike distance, from {1}:	6.2 miles
Hike distance, from {2}:	2 miles
Hike distance, from {3}:	4.4 miles
Cumulative ascent from {1}:	775 feet
Cumulative ascent from {2}:	400 feet
Cumulative ascent from {3}:	700 feet

Devil's Bridge Trail   Elevation Profile (from Waypoint {3})

Elevation (ft)

Distance (mi)

Doe Mountain Trail ★

Summary: The trail climbs up to and loops around the top of Doe Mountain, a true mesa with panoramic red rock views

Challenge Level: Moderate

Hiking Distance: About 2.6 miles round trip

Hiking Time: About 2 hours round trip

Trail Popularity:

Trailhead Directions: Parking for the Doe Mountain Trail is shared with the Bear Mountain Trail. From the "Y" roundabout (see page 5), drive west toward Cottonwood on SR 89A about 3 miles. Turn right onto Dry Creek Road (where speed limits are strictly enforced). Stay on Dry Creek Road to a stop sign (about 3 miles) then turn left onto Boynton Pass Road. Proceed about 1.6 miles to a stop sign. Turn left, continuing on Boynton Pass Road. The trailhead parking is the second one on the left side, about 1.75 miles from the stop sign {1}. The trailhead is at the south side of the parking area. There are toilets at the parking area.

Description: Hike southeast toward Doe Mountain where you'll soon intersect the Aerie Trail {2}. Just before you reach the rim, you'll pass through a narrow slot in the rocks. Once through the slot and on the mesa, turn around and look down at the parking area. Pay attention to where you came up {3} by observing your location relative to the parking area below because it can be hard to find the way back down after hiking around the top of Doe Mountain.

Although the top of Doe Mountain is crisscrossed with "social trails," the preferred way is to proceed straight across to the southern side of Doe Mountain then proceed in a clockwise direction around then back to the trail down. Another popular way is to go to the left then skirt the outer edge of the mountain for some great views {4} {5} {6} {7}. You may be bushwhacking a bit, so be sure to wear hiking boots to protect your ankles from the cactus and brush you'll be stepping over. The spectacular views are all around.

Note: The unmarked, unmaintained trail is difficult to follow at times. We strongly recommend using a portable GPS unit to hike around the top of Doe

Mountain and back to the trail to the parking area (go to https://greatsedonahikes.com/gps/gps.html).

Color Photos: Scan the QR code for color photos of this trail

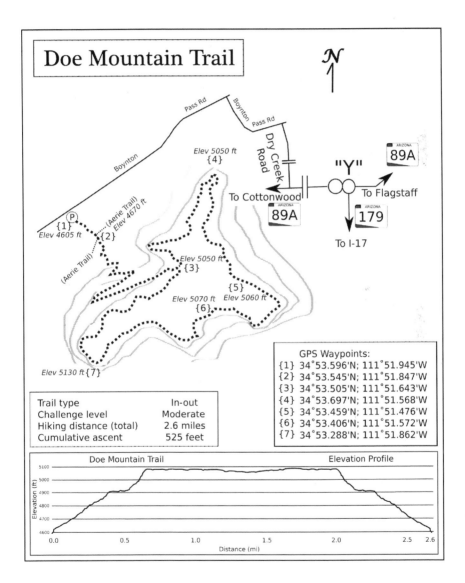

Doe Mountain Trail

Trail type	In-out
Challenge level	Moderate
Hiking distance (total)	2.6 miles
Cumulative ascent	525 feet

GPS Waypoints:
{1} 34°53.596'N; 111°51.945'W
{2} 34°53.545'N; 111°51.847'W
{3} 34°53.505'N; 111°51.643'W
{4} 34°53.697'N; 111°51.568'W
{5} 34°53.459'N; 111°51.476'W
{6} 34°53.406'N; 111°51.572'W
{7} 34°53.288'N; 111°51.862'W

Dry Creek Trail

Summary: An in-out hike that follows the path of Dry Creek through a forest

Challenge Level: Easy to Moderate, depending on length of hike

Hiking Distance: About 2.25 miles each way or 4.5 miles round trip

Hiking Time: About 2 ½ hours round trip

Trail Popularity: 👫

Trailhead Directions: From the "Y" roundabout (see page 5), drive west toward Cottonwood on SR 89A about 3 miles. Turn right onto Dry Creek Road (where speed limits are strictly enforced). Stay on Dry Creek Road for 2 miles then turn right onto Forest Road (FR) 152. Proceed to the end of FR 152 (about 4.5 miles) to the parking area on the left {1}. The parking area is the same as used for the Bear Sign and Vultee Arch Trails.

Note: FR 152 is an extremely rough road beyond the 0.2 mile paved section; a high clearance vehicle and 4WD are strongly recommended.

Description: This trail, which is at the northern edge of the Red Rock Secret Mountain Wilderness, follows the path cut by Dry Creek, crossing the dry creek bed about a dozen times. Because it is located at the end of the very rough FR 152, it isn't used very much and has become hard to follow in certain spots. We recommend you use a GPS loaded with the trail data (go to https://greatsedonahikes.com/gps/gps.html).

You'll be hiking in a northerly direction and intersect the Bear Sign Trail about 0.75 mile from the parking area {2}. The Dry Creek Trail is easy to follow here but pay attention when you cross the creek bed because the continuation of the trail on the other side isn't always obvious. As you continue, the canyon cut by Dry Creek gets narrower and you are treated to nice views of towering red rock formations, although some of the views are blocked by the stands of cypress and pines {3}. You'll come to a nice place for a snack after about 1.6 miles {4}. You can hike another 0.75 mile further up the creek bed if you like {5} but the trail becomes harder and harder to follow {6}.

Color Photos: Scan the QR code for color photos of this trail

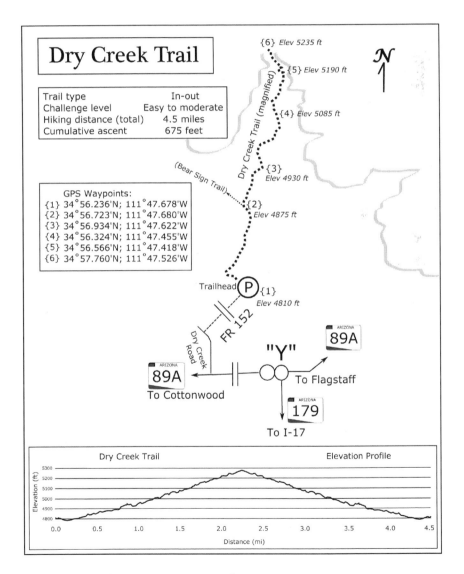

Fay Canyon Trail ★

Summary: A short, pleasant in-out stroll through a canyon with wonderful red rock views and an optional side trip to view a natural arch

Challenge Level: Easy for the Fay Canyon Trail; Moderate if you hike to Fay Canyon Arch

Hiking Distance: About 1.1 miles each way to the rock slide or 2.2 miles round trip. Add 0.5 mile round trip if you hike to Fay Canyon Arch or 2.7 miles round trip.

Hiking Time: About 1 ½ hours round trip

Trail Popularity:

Trailhead Directions: From the "Y" roundabout (see page 5), drive west toward Cottonwood on SR 89A about 3 miles. Turn right onto Dry Creek Road (where speed limits are strictly enforced). Stay on Dry Creek Road to a stop sign (about 3 miles) then turn left onto Boynton Pass Road. Proceed about 1.6 miles to a stop sign. Turn left, continuing on Boynton Pass Road. You park at the first parking area on the left side, about 0.8 miles from the stop sign {1}. The trailhead is across the road from the west end of the parking area. There are toilets at the parking area.

Description: Fay Canyon is one of our favorite trails for non-hiker guests because it is short (only about 2.2 miles round trip), relatively level, and very scenic. The trail essentially ends at a massive rock slide {4}.

And for those wanting a greater challenge, there is a side trail located about 0.5 mile from the main parking area that leads to a natural stone arch {2}. You'll have to scramble up about 225 feet on this unmarked trail if you want to see the arch, which is located up next to the cliff face {3}. This will add about 0.5 mile to the hike. This side trail is narrow and steep with cactus along the edges and loose rock so watch your footing. There is a narrow slot up under the arch where the rocks have separated and you can slip into the opening. Some people suggest that the area under the arch is a powerful vortex spot. (Additional information on vortexes can be found on page 144.)

Color Photos: Scan the QR code for color photos of this trail

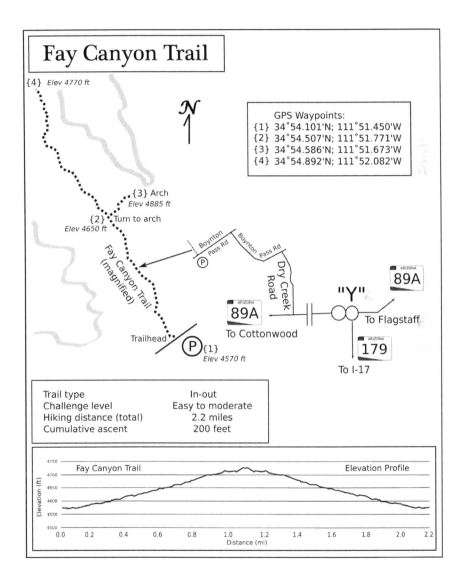

Fay Canyon Trail

{4} *Elev 4770 ft*

N

GPS Waypoints:
{1} 34°54.101'N; 111°51.450'W
{2} 34°54.507'N; 111°51.771'W
{3} 34°54.586'N; 111°51.673'W
{4} 34°54.892'N; 111°52.082'W

{3} Arch
Elev 4885 ft

{2} Turn to arch
Elev 4650 ft

Fay Canyon Trail (magnified)

Boynton Pass Rd

Boynton Pass Rd

P

Dry Creek Road

ARIZONA
89A

"Y"

ARIZONA
89A

To Flagstaff

Trailhead

P {1}
Elev 4570 ft

To Cottonwood

ARIZONA
179

To I-17

Trail type	In-out
Challenge level	Easy to moderate
Hiking distance (total)	2.2 miles
Cumulative ascent	200 feet

Fay Canyon Trail   Elevation Profile

Elevation (ft)

4750
4700
4650
4600
4550
4500

0.0 0.2 0.4 0.6 0.8 1.0 1.2 1.4 1.6 1.8 2.0 2.2
Distance (mi)

Hangover/Munds Wagon Loop

Summary: A loop or in-out hike around some large rock formations

Challenge Level: Moderate for the in-out hike, hard for the loop hike

Hiking Distance: About 3.2 miles in-out, 5.1 miles for the loop hike

Hiking Time: About 3 1/2 hours round trip

Trail Popularity: 👥👥

Trailhead Directions:
From the "Y" roundabout (see page 5), drive south on SR 179 about 0.3 mile to the Schnebly Hill Roundabout then drive 270 degrees (3/4 of the way) around to Schnebly Hill Road. Proceed 3.7 miles on Schnebly Hill. The trailhead parking is on your right {1}. Schnebly Hill is paved for the first mile but the last 2.7 miles is an unpaved road and can be very rough; a high clearance vehicle and 4WD are strongly recommended.

Description: This loop hike provides outstanding views but the trail is extremely difficult in places. You'll be hiking the Cow Pies Trail for the first 0.3 mile. Soon you'll pass by an area dotted with small black rocks, which are pieces of lava {2}. Some believe this to be another powerful vortex area. (Additional information on vortexes can be found on page 144.)

Instead of turning left to go to Cow Pies {3}, continue straight ahead to the base of Mitten Ridge. The trail turns left {4.} You'll soon come to a sign for the Hangover Trail {5}. As you continue west along the ridge, you'll have to follow the trail closely in some parts. The trail is very narrow with steep drop-offs in places. You'll be hiking on some narrow ledges so watch your footing. Watch for a sharp left turn about 0.2 mile beyond the "social trail" {6}. When you arrive at the saddle, which is at the west end of Mitten Ridge, you'll have a nice view of Midgley Bridge and Wilson Mountain to the north {7}. Return to the parking area from here for a 3.2 mile round trip hike.

To hike the loop, go to the east end of the ridge where you'll see the continuation of the Hangover Trail. You'll be hiking along a narrow trail with large drop-offs. The trail is off-camber and steep in many places so be extra careful. You'll come to several interesting hollows in another 0.2 mile {8}. As you continue, you are rewarded with outstanding views of Sedona but be sure to watch your footing. After a total of 4 miles, you'll intersect the Munds Wagon Trail {9}. Make a left turn here then follow Munds Wagon. After another 0.5 mile there is a "social trail" on your right that leads up to Schnebly Hill Road. Don't make the turn, but continue straight ahead then slightly to the left to stay on the main trail {10}. You'll cross Schnebly Hill Road after another 0.5 mile

{11} then shortly make a left turn {12} back to the parking area {1} for a 5.1 mile loop hike.

Note: Do not attempt this trail if it is wet or there is snow or ice on the trail. Be sure you have hiking boots with good traction. Do not attempt if you have a fear of heights or of narrow, steep trails with large drop-offs. Be aware of mountain bikers.

Color Photos: Scan the QR code for color photos of this trail

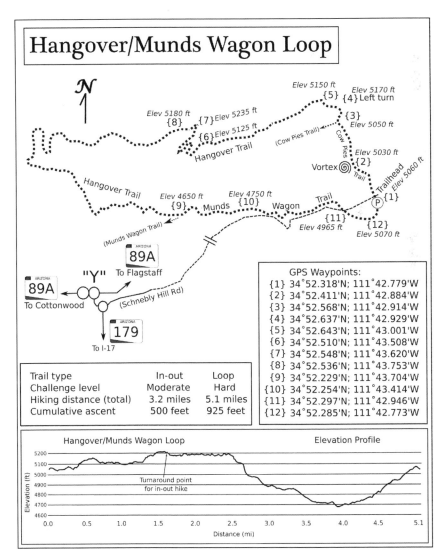

Hangover/Munds Wagon Loop

GPS Waypoints:
{1} 34°52.318'N; 111°42.779'W
{2} 34°52.411'N; 111°42.884'W
{3} 34°52.568'N; 111°42.914'W
{4} 34°52.637'N; 111°42.929'W
{5} 34°52.643'N; 111°43.001'W
{6} 34°52.510'N; 111°43.508'W
{7} 34°52.548'N; 111°43.620'W
{8} 34°52.536'N; 111°43.753'W
{9} 34°52.229'N; 111°43.704'W
{10} 34°52.254'N; 111°43.414'W
{11} 34°52.297'N; 111°42.946'W
{12} 34°52.285'N; 111°42.773'W

Trail type	In-out	Loop
Challenge level	Moderate	Hard
Hiking distance (total)	3.2 miles	5.1 miles
Cumulative ascent	500 feet	925 feet

Hangover/Munds Wagon Loop — Elevation Profile

69

HiLine Trail ★

Summary: An in-out or two-vehicle hike on a narrow trail that skirts the face of a red rock formation offering panoramic views of Sedona's red rocks.

Challenge Level:
Moderate

Hiking Distance: 2 miles each way to a great view of Cathedral Rock or 4 miles round trip; about 3.6 miles each way to the Baldwin Loop Trail or 7.2 miles round trip; 4.7 miles as a two-vehicle hike from the Yavapai Vista parking area to the Turkey Creek parking area

Hiking Time: About 2 hours to the great view of Cathedral Rock round trip; about 4 hours to the Baldwin Trail and return; about 2 ½ hours as a two vehicle hike to the Turkey Creek parking area from the Yavapai Vista parking area

Trail Popularity: 🚶🚶

Trailhead Directions: From the "Y" roundabout (see page 5), drive south on SR 179 about 4.8 miles to mile marker 308.5 then turn right into the Yavapai Vista parking area {1}. (Note: The Yavapai Vista parking area is accessible only from southbound SR 179.) For a two-vehicle hike, park the second vehicle at the Turkey Creek Trail parking area {14}, located 4 miles west on Verde Valley School Road (see Baldwin Loop).

Description: Hike past the interpretive signboard and around the metal railing then continue straight ahead where you will come to the intersection of the Kaibab and Yavapai Vista Trails {2}. Continue on the Kaibab Trail for 0.2 mile then turn left onto the Slim Shady Trail {3}. Hike about 0.2 mile to the beginning of the HiLine Trail on your right {4}.

The HiLine Trail is used by many bikers so you may encounter them on this narrow trail. The trail has a number of tight spots {5} so watch your footing. You'll have nice views of Courthouse Butte, Bell Rock, Lee Mountain, Rabbit Ears, and get your first view of Cathedral Rock after 1.2 miles from the parking area {6}. As you continue, the views of Cathedral Rock get better and better {7}. A good place to stop is 2 miles from the parking area {8}. We suggest you turn around here for a 4 mile round trip hike, but if you wish to hike further, make a right turn to begin the descent. After 0.4 mile the trail turns west at a cairn {9} You'll be crossing large expanses of slickrock for the next 0.6 mile. At 3 miles from the parking area, the trail begins a steep, slippery descent so watch your footing {10}. Shortly after the descent you'll be in a wash and as you continue you'll intersect the Baldwin Loop Trail in another 0.6 mile {11}. Turn around here for a 7.2 mile round trip hike, or turn left onto the Baldwin Trail, follow it for 0.6 mile then turn left (south) at the sign {12} for the trail to the Turkey Creek parking area {14}. In 400 feet, bear right {13} for a shortcut back to the Turkey Creek parking area {14}.

Note: This trail is narrow and uneven with large drop-offs – do not attempt it if there is snow or ice on the trail.

Color Photos: Scan the QR code for color photos of this trail

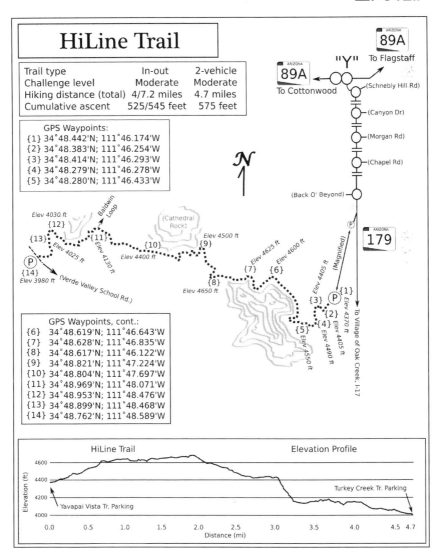

Honanki and Palatki Heritage Sites

Summary: A visit to two separate Sinagua pueblo ruins and rock art

Challenge Level: Easy

Hiking Distance: Honanki: About 0.25 mile each way or 0.5 mile round trip. Palatki: About 0.3 mile each way to the ruins or 0.6 mile round trip; add another 0.3 mile each way to the rock art or 0.6 mile round trip.

Hiking Time: About ¼ hour to and from each site but plan on at least an hour to view the ruins and rock art

Trail Popularity: Honanki 🚶🚶; Palatki 🚶🚶🚶🚶

Trailhead Directions: From the "Y" roundabout (see page 5), drive west toward Cottonwood on SR 89A about 3 miles. Turn right onto Dry Creek Road (where speed limits are strictly enforced) {1}. Stay on Dry Creek Road to a stop sign (about 3 miles) then turn left onto Boynton Pass Road {2}. Proceed about 1.6 miles to a stop sign. Turn left, continuing on Boynton Pass Road {3}. The road is paved for the first 2 miles then becomes gravel. Drive 4 miles to a stop sign then turn right onto Forest Road (FR) 525 {4}. After about 0.1 mile, take the left fork of FR 525 {5} for 4.5 miles to the Honanki parking area {7}. The right fork leads to Palatki in 1.75 miles {8}.

Note: These unpaved roads can be very rough so a high clearance vehicle is recommended. Pets are not allowed on either site.

Description: The Sinagua, ancestors of the Hopi, lived at Honanki and Palatki from about AD 1100 to 1300. Here they raised their families, made tools from stone, leather and wood, and hunted deer and rabbit.

Honanki: The Pink Jeep Company manages the Honanki (meaning Bear House) site. There are no volunteers or rangers stationed here. You are on your own to wander through the site. There is a metal rail fence to keep unauthorized folks out but you are very close to the structures. You may encounter people touring the site who are on jeep tours at the time you are there. The Pink Jeep Company asks that you not interfere with the tours.

Palatki: Palatki (meaning Red House) includes cliff dwellings, petroglyphs (etched markings) and pictographs (painted symbols). Because parking is limited at this Heritage Site, you must make a reservation by calling (928) 282-3854; however, there is no cost beyond the cost of a Red Rock Pass (or equivalent).

After you park at Palatki, walk to the Visitor Center and check in. Each trail is about 0.3 mile long. The trail to the cliff dwellings has about 75 rock steps and is steeper than the 15 step trail to the rock art. There are rangers and volunteers on duty to give the site's history and answer questions.

Color Photos: Scan the QR code for color photos of Honanki:

Color Photos: Scan the QR code for color photos of Palatki:

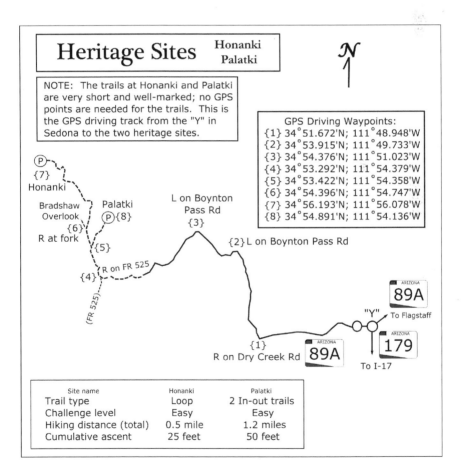

HS Canyon Trail

Summary: A pleasant in-out hike through a narrow, forested canyon

Challenge Level: Moderate

Hiking Distance: About 2.1 miles each way or 4.2 miles round trip

Hiking Time: About 2 ½ hours round trip

Trail Popularity: 🚶

Trailhead Directions: From the "Y" roundabout (see page 5), drive west toward Cottonwood on SR 89A about 3 miles. Turn right onto Dry Creek Road (where speed limits are strictly enforced). Stay on Dry Creek Road for 2 miles then turn right onto Forest Road (FR) 152. Proceed on FR 152 for 3.4 miles to the Secret Canyon parking area on your left {1}.

Note: FR 152 is an extremely rough road beyond the 0.2 mile paved section; a high clearance vehicle and 4WD are strongly recommended.

Description: To reach the HS Canyon Trail, you begin hiking the Secret Canyon Trail. You'll cross a wash after 0.6 mile {2}. Look to the right because after a rain there is a nice small pool of water. Proceed another 0.1 mile and you'll see the HS Canyon Trail #50 sign on your left {3}. The HS Canyon Trail gently rises about 625 feet providing good red rock views, although the forest of alligator junipers, oak and pinyon pines obscures most of them. You'll find a lot of manzanita along the trail. At higher elevations on the trail, more manzanita trees appear among the manzanita bushes. You'll come to a nice spot for a photo

74

after 1 mile {4}. As you proceed, the trail becomes somewhat overgrown – a result of its relative inaccessibility because of the poor condition of FR 152.

The name (HS Trail) reportedly comes from the early riders finding lots of horse s**t on this trail. When the Forest Service officially named the trail, they kept the initials (HS) but named it after Henry Schuerman, an early Sedona resident. The HS Canyon Trail is a good hike in the summer as there is plenty of shade. The trail ends next to Maroon Mountain {5}.

Color Photos: Scan the QR code for color photos of this trail

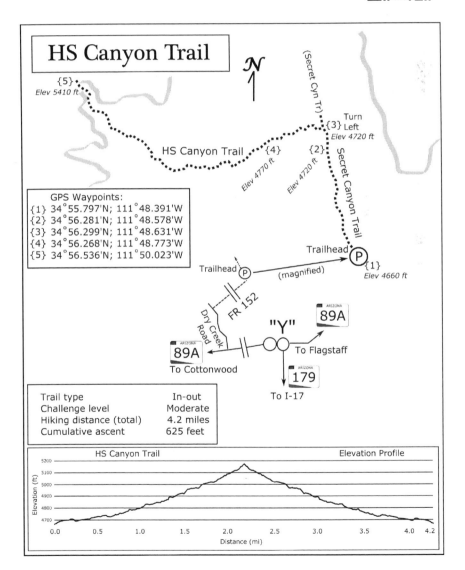

HS Canyon Trail

N

{5}
Elev 5410 ft

(Secret Cyn Trl)

HS Canyon Trail {4}
Elev 4770 ft

{2}
Elev 4720 ft

Turn
{3} Left
Elev 4720 ft

Secret Canyon Trail

GPS Waypoints:
{1} 34°55.797'N; 111°48.391'W
{2} 34°56.281'N; 111°48.578'W
{3} 34°56.299'N; 111°48.631'W
{4} 34°56.268'N; 111°48.773'W
{5} 34°56.536'N; 111°50.023'W

Trailhead
(magnified)

Trailhead (P)
{1}
Elev 4660 ft

Trailhead (P)

Dry Creek Road
FR 152

"Y"

ARIZONA 89A

ARIZONA 89A
To Cottonwood

To Flagstaff

ARIZONA 179
To I-17

Trail type	In-out
Challenge level	Moderate
Hiking distance (total)	4.2 miles
Cumulative ascent	625 feet

HS Canyon Trail — Elevation Profile

Elevation (ft): 5200, 5100, 5000, 4900, 4800, 4700

Distance (mi): 0.0 0.5 1.0 1.5 2.0 2.5 3.0 3.5 4.0 4.2

HT/Easy Breezy Loop

Summary: A partially shaded in-out or loop hike to the base of Cathedral Rock

Challenge Level:
Moderate

Hiking Distance: About 2.6 miles each way to the intersection of the Cathedral Rock Trail or 5.2 miles round trip; 5.1 miles as a loop hike

Hiking Time: About 3 ½ hours round trip

Trail Popularity:

Trailhead Directions:
From the "Y" roundabout (see page 5), drive south on SR 179 about 3.5 miles. You'll see a Scenic View and a hiking sign on the right side of SR 179 just past the Back O' Beyond roundabout. Turn left here then proceed across the median to the parking area {1}. The parking area for the HT Trail is the same as for the Bell Rock Pathway and Little Horse Trails. There are toilets at the parking area.

Description: You'll be hiking three trails to get to the base of Cathedral Rock. This is an alternate way of getting to Cathedral Rock if the Back O' Beyond parking area is full. You'll begin by hiking south on the Bell Rock Pathway. After 0.3 mile, you'll intersect the beginning of the Little Horse Trail {2}. Continue south for another 0.2 mile, and cross the footbridge. The HT Trail begins on your right {3}. As you hike along the HT Trail, you'll pass under both the northbound and southbound lanes of SR 179. There are pinyon pines in this area so you are partially shaded. Follow along the wash you crossed just before turning to the HT Trail. After 1.4 miles, you'll intersect the Easy Breezy Trail {4}. Continue on the HT Trail for another 0.3 mile then turn right onto the Templeton Trail {5}.

As you approach Cathedral Rock, the landscape changes to a desert environment so you'll see ocotillo plants, which likely will have their red blooms displayed in mid to late April. You'll intersect the west end of the Easy Breezy Trail at the 2.7 mile mark {6} and after another 0.1 mile, the Cathedral Rock Trail coming up from the parking area on the Back O' Beyond Road {7}. From here you can scramble up to the saddle of Cathedral Rock (see Cathedral Rock Trail).

For a loop hike, on the return trip turn onto the Easy Breezy Trail {6}. Follow it to the intersection with the HT Trail {4}. Turn left here to return to the parking area.

Color Photos: Scan the QR code for color photos of this trail

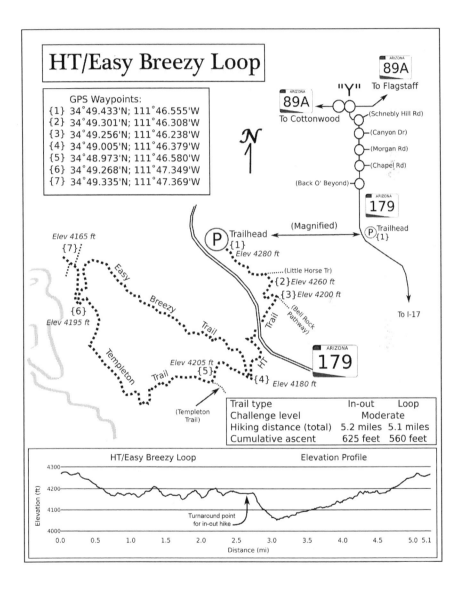

HT/Easy Breezy Loop

GPS Waypoints:
{1} 34°49.433'N; 111°46.555'W
{2} 34°49.301'N; 111°46.308'W
{3} 34°49.256'N; 111°46.238'W
{4} 34°49.005'N; 111°46.379'W
{5} 34°48.973'N; 111°46.580'W
{6} 34°49.268'N; 111°47.349'W
{7} 34°49.335'N; 111°47.369'W

ARIZONA 89A
"Y" To Flagstaff
ARIZONA 89A
To Cottonwood
(Schnebly Hill Rd)
(Canyon Dr)
(Morgan Rd)
(Chapel Rd)
(Back O' Beyond)
ARIZONA 179

Elev 4165 ft
{7}
Easy
Breezy
Trail
{6}
Elev 4195 ft
Templeton
Trail
Elev 4205 ft
{5}
(Templeton Trail)
(Magnified)
Trailhead
P {1}
Elev 4280 ft
(Little Horse Tr)
{2} Elev 4260 ft
{3} Elev 4200 ft
(Bell Rock Pathway)
HT
Trail
{4} Elev 4180 ft
ARIZONA 179
P Trailhead {1}
To I-17

Trail type	In-out	Loop
Challenge level	Moderate	
Hiking distance (total)	5.2 miles	5.1 miles
Cumulative ascent	625 feet	560 feet

HT/Easy Breezy Loop   Elevation Profile

Turnaround point for in-out hike

Elevation (ft): 4300, 4200, 4100, 4000
Distance (mi): 0.0 0.5 1.0 1.5 2.0 2.5 3.0 3.5 4.0 4.5 5.0 5.1

Huckaby Trail

Summary: An in-out or two-vehicle hike descending from Schnebly Hill Road to the banks of Oak Creek with a great view of Midgley Bridge

Challenge Level:
Moderate

Hiking Distance:
About 2.5 miles each way or 5 miles round trip; or 3 miles as a two-vehicle hike

Hiking Time:
About 3 hours round trip as an in-out hike; about 2 hours as a two vehicle hike

Trail Popularity:

Trailhead Directions: From the "Y" roundabout (see page 5), drive south on SR 179 about 0.3 mile to the Schnebly Hill roundabout then drive 270 degrees (3/4 of the way) around to Schnebly Hill Road. Proceed on the paved Schnebly Hill Road for 1 mile then turn left into the parking area {1}. The trailhead parking is shared with the Munds Wagon Trail. The trail begins on the west side of the parking area. There are toilets at the parking area. If you are doing a two-vehicle hike, park the other vehicle at the Midgley Bridge parking area (see Wilson Canyon Trail).

Description: The Huckaby Trail begins in a westerly direction from the parking area. You'll soon intersect the Marg's Draw Trail on the left {2}. Huckaby then turns north and crosses Bear Wallow Wash. The trail rises and falls as you approach Oak Creek Canyon. After about 0.7 mile, look for an overlook on the left {3} for a nice view of Uptown Sedona and Wilson Mountain. After about 1.6 miles, you'll have your first view of Midgley Bridge {4}. Look around for the views of Lucy, Snoopy, Cathedral Rock and many other named rock formations.

As you approach Oak Creek, the trail descends quite steeply {5}. At the 2 mile mark, you'll be down in the flood plain along Oak Creek where there is shade provided by the riparian trees. Watch for poison ivy along the trail. Unless the water is low and you want to cross to the other side of Oak Creek by doing some rock-hopping {7}, end the hike where you have an awesome view of Midgley Bridge, just north of Uptown Sedona {6}. If you continue across Oak Creek, you'll hike up about 150 feet then turn west to reach Midgley Bridge. You can make this hike a two-vehicle hike – one vehicle parked at the Schnebly Hill

Road parking area {1} and the other parked at Midgley Bridge {8}. Just make sure you can cross Oak Creek.

Note: There is no shade for the first 2 miles of this trail so it is a hot summer hike.

Color Photos: Scan the QR code for color photos of this trail

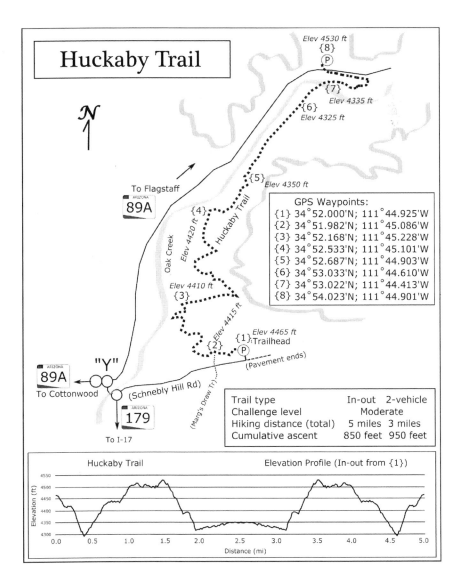

Huckaby Trail

Elev 4530 ft
{8}
Ⓟ

{7}

Elev 4335 ft
{6}
Elev 4325 ft

𝒩

To Flagstaff

89A ARIZONA

{5} Elev 4350 ft

{4} Huckaby Trail

Elev 4420 ft

Oak Creek

Elev 4410 ft
{3}

Elev 4415 ft

Elev 4465 ft
{1} Trailhead
{2} Ⓟ
(Pavement ends)

"Y"

89A ARIZONA
To Cottonwood

(Schnebly Hill Rd)

(Marg's Draw Tr)

179 ARIZONA

To I-17

GPS Waypoints:
{1} 34°52.000'N; 111°44.925'W
{2} 34°51.982'N; 111°45.086'W
{3} 34°52.168'N; 111°45.228'W
{4} 34°52.533'N; 111°45.101'W
{5} 34°52.687'N; 111°44.903'W
{6} 34°53.033'N; 111°44.610'W
{7} 34°53.022'N; 111°44.413'W
{8} 34°54.023'N; 111°44.901'W

Trail type	In-out 2-vehicle
Challenge level	Moderate
Hiking distance (total)	5 miles 3 miles
Cumulative ascent	850 feet 950 feet

Huckaby Trail   Elevation Profile (In-out from {1})

Elevation (ft)

4550
4500
4450
4400
4350
4300

0.0 0.5 1.0 1.5 2.0 2.5 3.0 3.5 4.0 4.5 5.0
Distance (mi)

Jim Thompson Trail

Summary: An in-out hike around the south edge of Steamboat Rock overlooking Midgley Bridge

Challenge Level: Moderate

Hiking Distance: About 2.7 miles each way or 5.4 miles round trip

Hiking Time: About 3 hours round trip

Trail Popularity: 🚶🚶

Trailhead Directions: From the "Y" roundabout (see page 5), drive north on SR 89A about 0.3 mile to Jordan Road. Turn left onto Jordan Road then drive to the end. Turn left onto West Park Ridge Drive then proceed through the paved cul-de-sac, continuing on the dirt road for 0.5 mile to the main parking area {1}. There are toilets at the parking area.

Description: Built by Jim Thompson in the 1880s as a road to a homestead at Indian Gardens, the trail begins on the northeast side of the parking area {2}. You'll begin by hiking north then quickly turn right and begin hiking south. After hiking 0.4 mile, you'll intersect the end of the Jordan Trail {3}. In another 0.3 mile, you'll come to an old gate frame. You'll be hiking in an easterly direction along Jim Thompson's old wagon road toward the base of Steamboat Rock.

There are excellent views to the north. The views to the south include Cathedral Rock and Uptown Sedona. Because you are looking into the sun, photographs to the south can be a challenge.

We usually stop after about 2.5 miles where you can see Midgley Bridge and look across Oak Creek Canyon {4}. If you continue on for about 0.25 mile, you'll intersect the Wilson Canyon Trail {5}after descending about 125 feet.

Note: There is only partial shade for about the first 0.5 mile and no shade after that so it can be a hot hike in the summer.

Color Photos: Scan the QR code for color photos of this trail

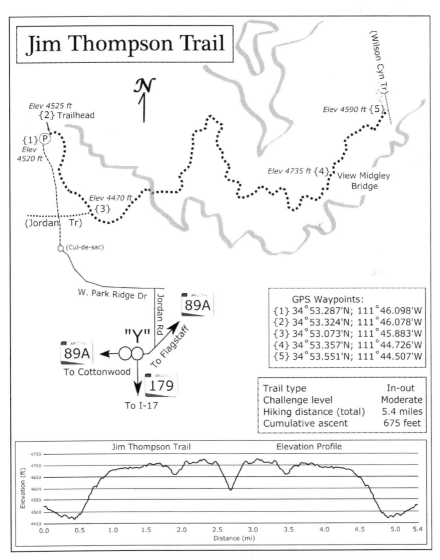

Jordan Trail

Summary: An in-out partially shaded hike near town that ends at the Soldier Pass Trail

Challenge Level: Easy to Moderate

Hiking Distance: About 1.6 miles each way or 3.2 miles round trip

Hiking Time: About 2 hours round trip

Trail Popularity: 🚶🚶🚶

Trailhead Directions: From the "Y" roundabout (see page 5), drive north on SR 89A about 0.3 mile to Jordan Road. Turn left onto Jordan Road then drive to the end. Turn left onto West Park Ridge Drive then proceed through the paved cul-de-sac. The road becomes dirt and you'll shortly come to a small parking area and an extension of the Jordan Trail on the left {2}. We recommend you continue on another 0.4 mile to the main parking area. There are toilets at the main parking area. The trailhead at the main parking area is on the west side, next to the toilets.

Description: If you begin the trail from the main parking area, you'll hike a short distance to the west, then turn south. After 0.4 mile, you'll intersect a sign for the Jordan Trail {3}. Turn right (west) then begin hiking the main trail somewhat uphill as you hike along an old road. If you turn left (east), you'll cross the road then intersect the Jim Thompson Trail after 0.2 mile.

The views gradually improve as you continue the hike. You'll intersect the Javelina Trail after another 0.3 mile {4}, intersect the Ant Hill Trail and then intersect the Cibola Trail at the 1.4 mile mark {5}. Continue on the Jordan Trail until you intersect the Soldier Pass Trail at Devil's Kitchen, which is the largest sinkhole in the Sedona area {6}.

If you want to continue a little further, hike north on the Soldier Pass Trail for 0.4 mile to the Seven Sacred Pools {7}. You can retrace your route or hike back on the Cibola Trail to the parking area. The Jordan Trail is popular with mountain bicyclists so you may encounter them on the trail.

Color Photos: Scan the QR code for color photos of this trail

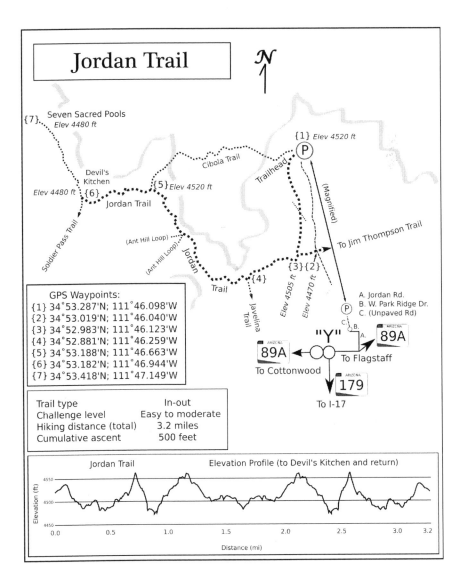

Jordan Trail

N

{7} Seven Sacred Pools
Elev 4480 ft

{1} Elev 4520 ft
P

Cibola Trail

Devil's
Kitchen
Elev 4480 ft {6}
{5} Elev 4520 ft

Jordan Trail

Trailhead

(Magnified)

To Jim Thompson Trail

Soldier Pass Trail

(Ant Hill Loop)

(Ant Hill Loop)

Jordan

{3} {2}
{4}
Elev 4505 ft
Elev 4470 ft

Trail

Javelina Trail

P
C B.

A. Jordan Rd.
B. W. Park Ridge Dr.
C. (Unpaved Rd)

A. 89A

GPS Waypoints:
{1} 34°53.287'N; 111°46.098'W
{2} 34°53.019'N; 111°46.040'W
{3} 34°52.983'N; 111°46.123'W
{4} 34°52.881'N; 111°46.259'W
{5} 34°53.188'N; 111°46.663'W
{6} 34°53.182'N; 111°46.944'W
{7} 34°53.418'N; 111°47.149'W

"Y"
89A ←
→ To Flagstaff
To Cottonwood

179
To I-17

Trail type	In-out
Challenge level	Easy to moderate
Hiking distance (total)	3.2 miles
Cumulative ascent	500 feet

Jordan Trail   Elevation Profile (to Devil's Kitchen and return)

Elevation (ft)
4550
4500
4450
0.0   0.5   1.0   1.5   2.0   2.5   3.0   3.2
Distance (mi)

Kelly Canyon Trail

Summary: A pleasant, shaded in-out hike in a ponderosa pine forest with interesting rocks and cliffs

Challenge Level: Easy to Moderate

Hiking Distance: About 3 miles each way or 6 miles round trip

Hiking Time: About 3 hours round trip

Trail Popularity: 🚶

Trailhead Directions: From the "Y" roundabout (see page 5), drive north on SR 89A about 17.5 miles. When you reach mile marker 391, look for a brown sign with the numbers 237 on it. In about 0.3 mile, turn right onto Forest Road 237 {1}, located 1.5 miles beyond the Oak Creek Vista. Follow the dirt road about 1 mile. Just past the Designated Dispersed Campsites 401-426 sign on the right, you'll be alongside a rustic fence where you'll see a yellow sign with a left arrow ahead. Park along the fence off the road (to let traffic get by your vehicle) then walk up to the yellow sign {2}. Climb over the fence then walk down the primitive road. Continue in the same direction for about 500 feet until you go over the bank and down into Pumphouse Wash {3}. Be careful and watch your footing as you hike down as it is steep with loose rocks. Continue east then hike through the opening in the rocks ahead of you for another 500 feet to the beginning of the trail (see photo above) {4}.

Description: This trail takes you across Pumphouse Wash then up Kelly Canyon which is thickly forested and shady. It is a very peaceful and beautiful hike, although you won't find red rock views here. You'll be climbing over several downed trees. There are interesting rock formations as you travel along with many wildflowers in the summer. At 0.8 mile, you'll make a left turn then scramble down about 30 feet into the wash {5} to follow the trail. As you continue, you'll be climbing over and around trees that have fallen across the trail. The trail is seldom used but you shouldn't have trouble following it. Bear left at the fork located about 1.25 miles in {6}. You'll come to a downed tree after another 0.3 mile {7}. You'll intersect several "social trails" along the way {8} {9}. After hiking a total of 3 miles, you'll intersect FR 237 {9}.

The ambient temperature you encounter on this trail will be about 10 degrees cooler than in Sedona because of the elevation (about 6400 feet) and the shade provided by the trees. It is a pleasant summer hike, but watch for poison ivy, especially in the wash beyond {5}.

Color Photos: Scan the QR code for color photos of this trail

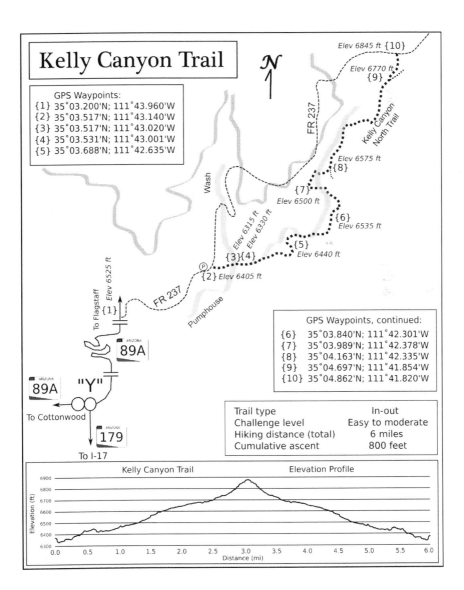

Little Horse Trail ★

Summary: A lovely in-out hike to Chicken Point, a large slickrock knoll with majestic views

Challenge Level: Moderate

Hiking Distance: About 2 miles each way or 4 miles round trip

Hiking Time: About 2 hours round trip

Trail Popularity: 🚶🚶🚶🚶🚶

Trailhead Directions: From the "Y" roundabout (see page 5), drive south on SR 179 about 3.5 miles. You'll see a Scenic View and a hiking sign on the right side of SR 179 just past the Back O' Beyond roundabout. Turn left here then proceed across the median to the parking area {1}. There are toilets at the parking area.

Description: You'll begin by hiking south on the Bell Rock Pathway for 0.3 mile until it intersects the beginning of the Little Horse Trail {2}. Turn left here to begin the Little Horse Trail. When you come to a dry wash, turn left to cross the wash then follow the trail east then north toward the Twin Buttes, an impressive red rock formation. After about 1 mile, you'll intersect the Llama Trail on the right {3}. You will intersect the Chapel Trail at the 1.4 mile mark {4}. If you have the time, follow the Chapel Trail for 0.5 mile until it intersects Chapel Road to go up to visit the Chapel of the Holy Cross {5}. Returning to the Little Horse Trail, continue on for another 0.4 mile where you'll arrive at an expansive area of slickrock known as Chicken Point. The climb up to Chicken

86

Point isn't hard and is well worth the effort {6}. Chicken Point is named for thrill-seeking jeep drivers who once dared to drive close to the edge of the point (jeep access is no longer permitted on Chicken Point). If you look to the south, you'll see a chicken-shaped rock high up on the red rock cliff. Chicken Point is a nice place for a snack break as the views are outstanding. You'll likely encounter some Pink Jeeps as the Broken Arrow tour brings many visitors to this beautiful area.

Color Photos: Scan the QR code for color photos of this trail

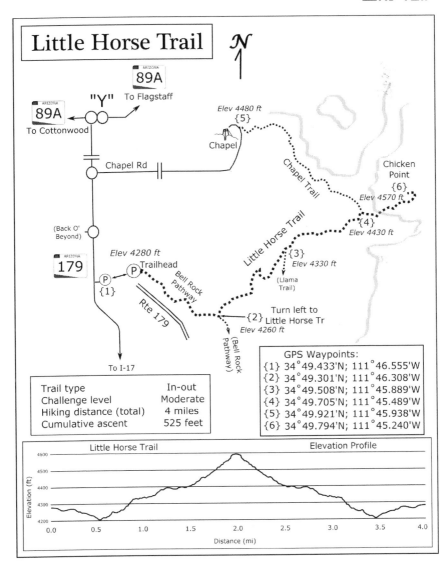

Llama/Baby Bell Loop

Summary: A short loop hike with panoramic views of many of Sedona's famous rock formations

Challenge Level: Easy

Hiking Distance: About 1.3 miles

Hiking Time: About 1 hour round trip

Trail Popularity:

Trailhead Directions:
From the "Y" roundabout (see page 5), drive south on SR 179 for about 5 miles to the parking area. After you drive about 3.2 miles, just past the Back O' Beyond roundabout, SR 179 becomes a divided highway. Continue driving south. About 1.8 miles beyond the Back O' Beyond roundabout, southbound SR 179 adds a passing lane on the left. From the passing lane, turn left at the sign for the Court House Vista parking area {1} (it's the second scenic view on the left side of SR 179). Before you turn, you'll see Bell Rock ahead of you on the left side of SR 179. There are toilets at the parking area. The trail starts on the southeast side of the parking area.

Description: This is a scenic, short loop we like to hike in a clockwise direction, although you can also hike it in the counterclockwise direction. The trails you'll be hiking are a favorite of mountain bicyclists so you may encounter some. From the Court House Vista parking area, look for the Phone Trail on your left about 25 feet past the interpretive signboard. Turn left onto the Phone Trail and you'll see Baby Bell rock on the left. Follow the Phone Trail 0.3 mile then continue north on the Bell Rock Pathway Trail {2} for another 0.1 mile then turn right onto the Baby Bell Trail {3}.

Soon after beginning the Baby Bell Trail, you'll see Rabbit Ears straight ahead. You'll come to a signpost at 0.5 mile where you'll make a right turn to continue on the Baby Bell Trail {4}. Look to the west here for a great view of Cathedral Rock. At 0.7 mile, you'll intersect the Llama Trail and have great red rock views all around {5}. Make a right turn here then continue on the Llama Trail. At 0.8 mile, you'll intersect the Courthouse Butte Loop Trail {6}. Make a right turn then follow Courthouse Butte Loop for 0.1 mile. Continue on the Bell Rock Pathway {7}. At 1.2 miles, you'll intersect the Bell Rock Trail {8}. Turn right here then follow the Bell Rock Trail back to the parking area {1} to complete the loop. There isn't much shade on this trail so it would be a good choice in cooler weather.

Color Photos: Scan the QR code for color photos of this trail

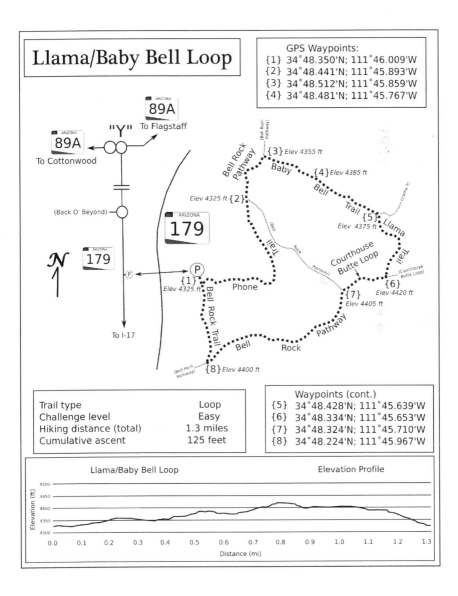

Llama/Baby Bell Loop

GPS Waypoints:
{1} 34°48.350'N; 111°46.009'W
{2} 34°48.441'N; 111°45.893'W
{3} 34°48.512'N; 111°45.859'W
{4} 34°48.481'N; 111°45.767'W

Trail type	Loop
Challenge level	Easy
Hiking distance (total)	1.3 miles
Cumulative ascent	125 feet

Waypoints (cont.)
{5} 34°48.428'N; 111°45.639'W
{6} 34°48.334'N; 111°45.653'W
{7} 34°48.324'N; 111°45.710'W
{8} 34°48.224'N; 111°45.967'W

Llama/Bail Loop or Llama/Little Horse Loop

Summary: A loop hike with panoramic views of many of Sedona's famous rock formations

Challenge Level: Easy to Moderate

Hiking Distance: About 4.4 miles for the Llama/ Bail/Bell Rock Pathway loop; about 6 miles for the Llama/ Little Horse/Bell Rock Pathway/Phone Trail loop

Hiking Time: About 3 hours round trip for the Llama/Little Horse/Bell Rock Pathway/Phone Trail Loop

Trail Popularity: 🚶🚶 🚶🚶 🚶🚶

Trailhead Directions: From the "Y" roundabout (see page 5), drive south on SR 179 for about 5 miles to the parking area. After you drive about 3.2 miles, just past the Back O' Beyond roundabout, SR 179 becomes a divided highway. Continue driving south. About 1.8 miles beyond the Back O' Beyond roundabout, southbound SR 179 adds a passing lane on the left. From the passing lane, turn left at the sign for the Court House Vista parking area {1} (it's the second scenic view on the left side of SR 179). Before you turn, you'll see Bell Rock ahead of you on the left side of SR 179. There are toilets at the parking area. The trail starts on the southeast side of the parking area. There is another Llama trailhead off of the Little Horse Trail {8}.

Description: The Llama Trail goes from Bell Rock to the Little Horse Trail. It is a favorite of mountain bicyclists. We prefer to hike it as a loop hike. From the parking area, proceed past the interpretive signboard then follow the Bell Rock Trail 0.1 mile to the intersection with the Bell Rock Pathway {2}. Turn left (northeast) at the sign that says, To Courthouse Butte Loop then follow the Bell Rock Pathway 0.3 mile. Continue straight ahead onto the Courthouse Butte Loop Trail {3}. Follow Courthouse Butte Loop for about 300 feet then turn left onto the Llama Trail {4}.

In 1 mile, you'll come to a scenic area with 8 depressions in the slickrock that are usually filled with water {5}. Continue another 0.9 mile to the intersection with the Bail Trail {6}. You can turn left here then follow the Bail Trail 0.4 mile

90

to the intersection with the Bell Rock Pathway {7}, or continue 1.1 miles on the Llama Trail to the Little Horse Trail {8} then turn left to reach the Bell Rock Pathway {9}. Hike south on the Bell Rock Pathway then turn onto the Phone Trail {10} for a shortcut back to the parking area. The Llama Trail approaches Lee Mountain and provides outstanding views of Bell Rock, Courthouse Butte, Twin Buttes and Cathedral Rock. There isn't much shade on this trail so it would be a good choice in cooler weather.

Color Photos: Scan the QR code for color photos of this trail

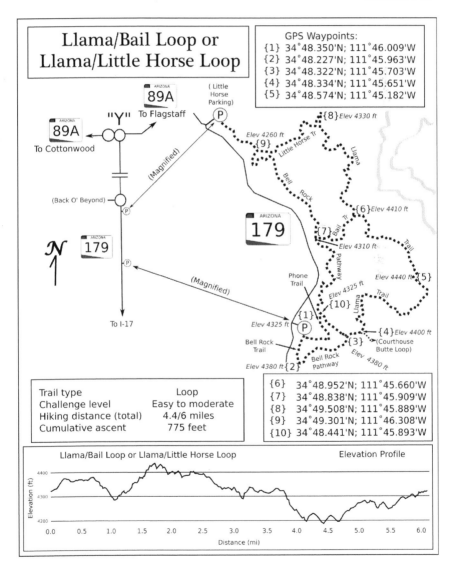

Long Canyon Trail

Summary: An in-out hike through a forested canyon with some good red rock views

Challenge Level: Moderate

Hiking Distance: About 3.5 miles each way or 7 miles round trip

Hiking Time: About 3 ½ hours round trip

Trail Popularity: 👣 👣

Trailhead Directions: From the "Y" roundabout (see page 5), drive west toward Cottonwood on SR 89A about 3 miles. Turn right onto Dry Creek Road (where speed limits are strictly enforced). Stay on Dry Creek Road to a stop sign (about 3 miles) then turn right onto Long Canyon Road. Proceed 0.6 mile to the parking area on the left {1}. The trailhead is at the parking area.

Description: This is a nice moderate partially shaded trail through a canyon with red rock views, although some are obstructed. The first 0.75 mile is an old jeep trail. This part of the trail is not shaded and can be very hot in the summer. But once you are in the forest, the trees provide shade. You'll make a left turn after 0.4 mile {2} and come to a Long Canyon sign at 0.6 mile. You intersect the Deadman's Pass Trail after about 1 mile {3}. Soon you'll see the Seven Canyons golf course and subdivision on the right. As you continue, the trail becomes more shaded and you'll cross several washes. We suggest you continue to hike Long Canyon for another 2 miles then begin the return trip {4}.

Color Photos: Scan the QR code for color photos of this trail

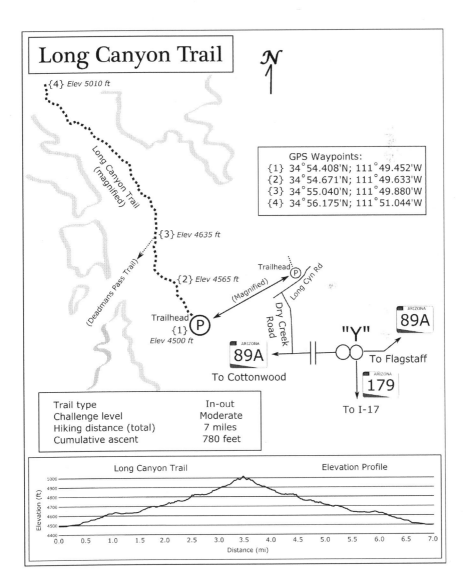

Long Canyon Trail

N

{4} *Elev 5010 ft*

Long Canyon Trail (magnified)

GPS Waypoints:
{1} 34°54.408'N; 111°49.452'W
{2} 34°54.671'N; 111°49.633'W
{3} 34°55.040'N; 111°49.880'W
{4} 34°56.175'N; 111°51.044'W

{3} *Elev 4635 ft*

(Deadmans Pass Trail)

Trailhead
(Magnified)

{2} *Elev 4565 ft*

Long Cyn Rd

Trailhead
{1}
Elev 4500 ft

Dry Creek Road

"Y"

89A

ARIZONA 89A

To Flagstaff

To Cottonwood

179

To I-17

Trail type	In-out
Challenge level	Moderate
Hiking distance (total)	7 miles
Cumulative ascent	780 feet

Long Canyon Trail   Elevation Profile

Elevation (ft)

5000
4900
4800
4700
4600
4500
4400

0.0 0.5 1.0 1.5 2.0 2.5 3.0 3.5 4.0 4.5 5.0 5.5 6.0 6.5 7.0

Distance (mi)

Marg's Draw Trail

Summary: An in-out hike with great red rock views

Challenge Level:
Easy to Moderate

Hiking Distance:
About 1.3 miles each way from the Sombart Lane trailhead to Schnebly Hill Road or 2.6 miles round trip; about 2.1 miles each way from the Morgan Road trailhead to Schnebly Hill Road or 4.2 miles round trip

Hiking Time: About 1 ½ hours from Sombart Lane to Schnebly Hill Road round trip; about 2 hours from Morgan Road to Schnebly Hill Road round trip

Trail Popularity: 👫👫

Trailhead Directions: There are actually three trailheads for this trail: At the south end, at the north end and in the middle of the trail. The south trailhead is at the end of Morgan Road and is shared with the Broken Arrow Trail. From the "Y" roundabout (see page 5), drive south on SR 179 1.5 miles to the roundabout at Morgan Road. Turn left (east) onto Morgan Road then drive about 0.6 mile to the trailhead parking on your left (the last part is a dirt road) {1}.

The north trailhead is located on Schnebly Hill Road. From the "Y" roundabout, drive south on SR 179 about 0.3 mile to the Schnebly Hill roundabout then drive 270 degrees (3/4 of the way) around to Schnebly Hill Road. Proceed on the paved Schnebly Hill Road for 1 mile then turn left into the parking area {5}. This parking area is shared with the Huckaby and Mund's Wagon Trails. There are toilets at this parking area. Hike west on the Huckaby Trail for about 0.2 mile then turn left onto the Marg's Draw Trail {5}.

The middle trailhead is at the end of Sombart Lane, which is located 0.7 mile south of the "Y" off of SR 179 {3}.

Description: The trail essentially goes north and south, parallel with SR 179. You'll encounter a number of "social trails" along the way. For example, about 0.8 mile north of the Broken Arrow trailhead, be sure you take the main trail to the northeast rather than the "social trail" to the west at this intersection {2}. The photo shows this intersection and the hikers making the correct trail choice. Hiking from the middle trailhead is steep for the first 0.1 mile then is relatively flat {4}. The trail is close to town so there are residences at either end. But in the middle you are in wilderness and have the feeling of being away from it all. You'll have nice views of Snoopy and Lucy rock formations.

Color Photos: Scan the QR code for color photos of this trail

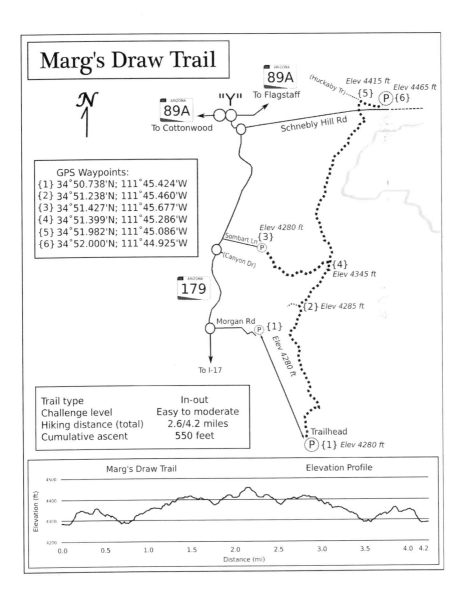

Marg's Draw Trail

GPS Waypoints:
{1} 34°50.738'N; 111°45.424'W
{2} 34°51.238'N; 111°45.460'W
{3} 34°51.427'N; 111°45.677'W
{4} 34°51.399'N; 111°45.286'W
{5} 34°51.982'N; 111°45.086'W
{6} 34°52.000'N; 111°44.925'W

Trail type	In-out
Challenge level	Easy to moderate
Hiking distance (total)	2.6/4.2 miles
Cumulative ascent	550 feet

Mayan Maiden Trail

Summary: An in-out hike to observe a unique rock formation and great red rock views

Challenge Level: Moderate

Hiking Distance: About 1.25 miles each way or 2.5 miles round trip

Hiking Time: About 1 ½ hours round trip

Trail Popularity:

Trailhead Directions: From the "Y" roundabout (see page 5), drive south on SR 179 about 7 miles to the Jacks Canyon and Verde Valley School Road roundabout then turn right (west) onto Verde Valley School Road. Drive 2 miles to the parking area on the left {1}. The trail begins across the road.

Description: This moderate hike begins on Verde Valley School Road and is a narrow, unmarked trail used primarily by cyclists. There are places that are moderately steep with loose rock and sand so watch your footing. In 0.1 mile, turn right near the telephone pole {2} then at 0.2 mile turn left to follow the trail {3}. Look to the right for a very unique rock hoodoo which has a very unusual shape (see photo above). You'll pass alongside a fence then come to a nice view at 0.4 mile {4} then another at 0.5 mile {5}. Here you turn left then begin climbing.

As you climb higher, you are rewarded with some spectacular views of the Village of Oak Creek, the green fairways of the Oak Creek Country Club and Cathedral Rock in the distance.

At 0.85 mile, you'll climb up some natural limestone steps {6} where you'll begin to hike north then east around an unnamed rock formation. At 1.1 miles, the trail splits {7}. Take the right fork here to continue on to two nice overlooks {8} {9} of Big Park and the Oak Creek Country Club below.

If you want to take a slightly different path on the return trip, turn right about 50 feet before you reach waypoint {3}. This trail also takes you back to the parking area.

Color Photos: Scan the QR code for color photos of this trail

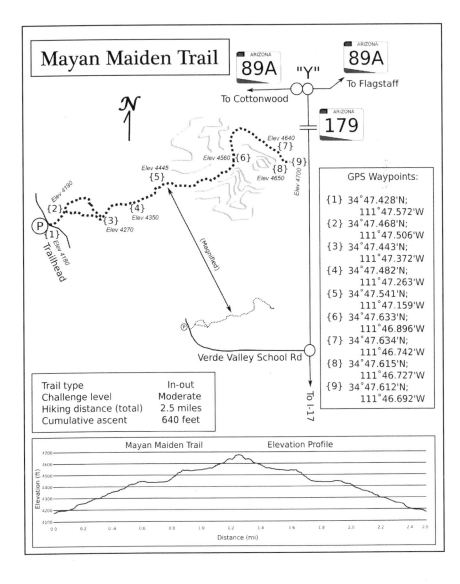

Mayan Maiden Trail

89A "Y"

89A ARIZONA

ARIZONA

To Cottonwood

To Flagstaff

ARIZONA
179

𝒩

Elev 4640 {7}
Elev 4560 {6}
Elev 4445 {5}
{9}
{8}
Elev 4650
Elev 4700
{2}
{4}
{3} Elev 4350
Elev 4270
Elev 4190
{1}
P
Elev 4180
Trailhead

(Magnified)

P

Verde Valley School Rd

To I-17

GPS Waypoints:

{1} 34°47.428'N;
111°47.572'W
{2} 34°47.468'N;
111°47.506'W
{3} 34°47.443'N;
111°47.372'W
{4} 34°47.482'N;
111°47.263'W
{5} 34°47.541'N;
111°47.159'W
{6} 34°47.633'N;
111°46.896'W
{7} 34°47.634'N;
111°46.742'W
{8} 34°47.615'N;
111°46.727'W
{9} 34°47.612'N;
111°46.692'W

Trail type	In-out
Challenge level	Moderate
Hiking distance (total)	2.5 miles
Cumulative ascent	640 feet

Mayan Maiden Trail   Elevation Profile

Elevation (ft)

4700
4600
4500
4400
4300
4200
4100

0.0 0.2 0.4 0.6 0.8 1.0 1.2 1.4 1.6 1.8 2.0 2.2 2.4 2.5

Distance (mi)

Mescal/Long Canyon Loop ★

Summary: An in-out hike that skirts the base of Mescal Mountain with both panoramic and up close red rock views with the option for a loop hike

Challenge Level:
Easy to Moderate.

Hiking Distance:
About 2.4 miles each way to the Deadman's Pass Trail intersection or 4.8 miles round trip; about 5 miles for Mescal Trail to Deadman's Pass Trail to Long Canyon Trail loop

Hiking Time: About 2 ½ hours for the in-out hike to Deadman's Pass Trail round trip; about 3 hours for the Long Canyon loop round trip

Trail Popularity: 🚶🚶🚶

Trailhead Directions: From the "Y" roundabout (see page 5), drive west toward Cottonwood on SR 89A about 3 miles. Turn right onto Dry Creek Road (where speed limits are strictly enforced). Stay on Dry Creek Road to a stop sign (about 3 miles) then turn right onto Long Canyon Road. Proceed 0.3 mile to the parking area on the right and park at the northeast (far) end {1}. The trail begins across the road from the northeast end of the parking area.

Description: This is a favorite trail that provides both close-up and distant red rock views. After the first 0.1 mile, the trail begins to gently rise as you approach the base of Mescal Mountain. At 0.25 mile, you'll intersect the connector trail to Long Canyon Trail on your right {2}. Continue straight ahead. At 0.4 mile, you are on the top of a high bluff with good red rock views all around. You'll pass a cairn and trail marker for the Yucca Trail {3} then at the 1 mile mark, look up high to the right where you'll observe a large cave in the side of Mescal Mountain {4}. Soon the trail becomes very narrow in places with steep drop offs – watch your footing. You'll find signs indicating Difficult and Extreme portions of the trail for the mountain bikers. We recommend you hike the Difficult path. After 1.75 miles, you'll come to a cairn and trail marker for the Canyon of Fools Trail [5]. Just beyond you can see Kachina Woman in Boynton Canyon, Cockscomb, Doe Mountain, Bear Mountain and Courthouse Butte in the distance.

As you proceed, the views get better and better. At 2.2 miles [6], the trail begins to descend some 85 feet in 0.25 mile to intersect the Deadman's Pass Trail [7]. Turn around here or, if you wish to hike a loop, turn right onto the Deadman's Pass Trail then hike for 0.9 mile to the Long Canyon Trail. Turn right onto the Long Canyon Trail {8} then follow it back toward Long Canyon Road. You'll see a connector trail just before the parking area on Long Canyon Road {9}. Turn right to follow the connector trail back to the Mescal Trail. Turn left when you reach the intersection with the Mescal Trail {2} to return to the parking area {1}.

Note: Don't attempt this trail if it is snowy or the trail is icy. There are some places where the trail is narrow with drop offs on the side.

Color Photos: Scan the QR code for color photos of this trail

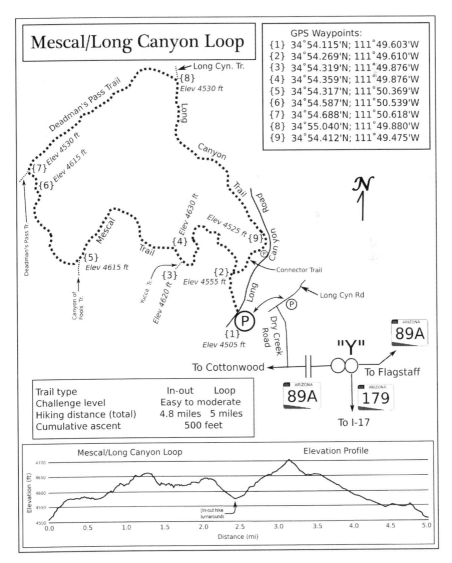

Trail type	In-out	Loop
Challenge level	Easy to moderate	
Hiking distance (total)	4.8 miles	5 miles
Cumulative ascent	500 feet	

Munds Wagon Trail

Summary: An in-out hike following an old wagon road and stream bed parallel to Schnebly Hill Road

Challenge Level: Moderate

Hiking Distance: About 2.8 miles each way or 5.6 miles round trip

Hiking Time: About 3 hours round trip

Trail Popularity: 🚶🚶

Trailhead Directions: From the "Y" roundabout (see page 5), drive south on SR 179 about 0.3 mile to the Schnebly Hill Roundabout then drive 270 degrees (3/4 of the way) around to Schnebly Hill Road. Proceed on Schnebly Hill Road for 1 mile then turn left into the parking area {1}. If you start driving on the unpaved Schnebly Hill Road, you've missed the trailhead. Turn around and go back. The trail begins on the east side of the parking area. The trailhead parking is shared with the Huckaby and Marg's Draw Trails. There are toilets at the parking area.

Description: This partially shaded trail follows an old wagon road along Schnebly Hill Road. Shortly after you start out, you'll cross Schnebly Hill Road, hike a short distance then cross back over. If you have a snack with you, there are picnic tables about 1.2 miles from the parking area {2}. At 1.8 miles, you'll intersect the Hangover Trail on your left {3}. At 2.1 miles, there is a "social trail" on your right that leads up to Schnebly Hill Road. Don't make the turn here, but continue straight ahead and slightly to the left to stay on the main trail

100

{4}. After about 2.5 miles {5} you'll be looking up at the Cow Pies (see Cow Pies Trail). Continue on another 0.3 mile where you'll cross Schnebly Hill Road {6} then make a left {7} to go to the Cow Pies Trail parking area.

The trail is much prettier when there is water flowing from snow runoff, which usually happens in the spring.

Color Photos: Scan the QR code for color photos of this trail

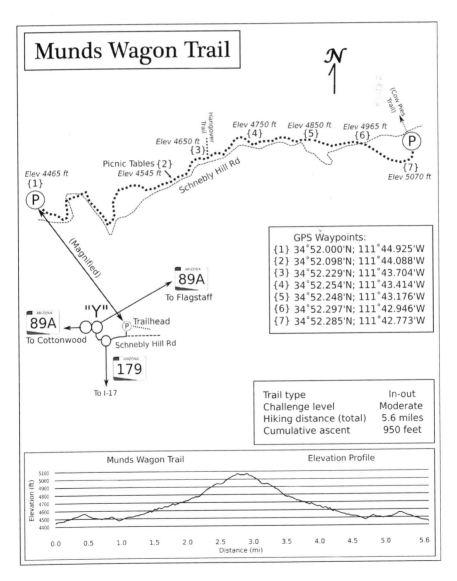

Old Post/Carroll Canyon Loop

Summary: A loop hike using a series of connected trails west of Sedona featuring some nice views but with little shade

Challenge Level: Moderate

Hiking Distance: About 5 miles round trip for the Old Post/Carroll Canyon loop hike

Hiking Time: About 2½ hours round trip

Trail Popularity: 🚶🚶

Trailhead Directions: From the "Y" roundabout (see page 5), drive west toward Cottonwood on SR 89A about 4.25 miles. Turn left onto Upper Red Rock Loop Road. You'll pass Sedona High School on your right. Continue for 1.8 miles then turn left onto Chavez Ranch Road. Drive 0.2 miles to the parking

area on the left {1}. There is room for about 8 vehicles. The trail begins at the parking area.

Description: You'll begin by following an old road, used for mail delivery long ago. After hiking 0.3 mile, you'll intersect the Ramshead Trail on the right {2} and the Herkenham Trail to the left at 0.7 mile mark {3}. Periodically look behind you for some nice views of Cathedral Rock and Courthouse Butte. You'll come to the southern intersection with the Carroll Canyon Trail at the 1 mile mark {4}. Stay on the Old Post Trail rather than turn onto the Carroll Canyon Trail (you'll be back to this point on your return hike).

Hike for an additional 0.4 mile and you'll intersect the Skywalker Trail on the left {5}. The trail begins a gradual descent here and you'll have a nice view of Thunder Mountain ahead. After hiking 2.2 miles from the parking area, you'll intersect the north end of the Carroll Canyon Trail {6}. Turn right onto the Carroll Canyon Trail here.

The Ridge Trail joins the Carroll Canyon Trail after another 0.6 mile {7}; they are a combined trail for 0.2 mile {8}. When they split, stay on the Carroll Canyon Trail. After hiking 4 miles from the parking area, you'll be back at the southern intersection of the Carroll Canyon and Old Post Trails {4}. Turn left onto the Old Post Trail here then hike 1 mile to the parking area {1}.

We've seen many wildflowers on these trails in late April and early May.

Note: There is very little shade on this hike so it would be a good choice in cooler weather.

Color Photos: Scan the QR code for color photos of this trail

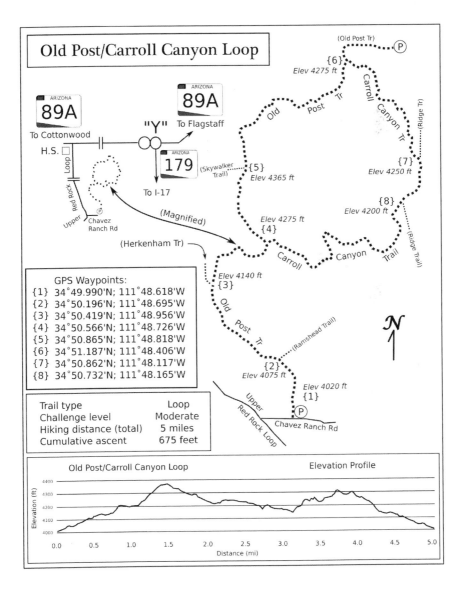

Old Post/Carroll Canyon Loop

| GPS Waypoints: |
| {1} 34°49.990'N; 111°48.618'W |
| {2} 34°50.196'N; 111°48.695'W |
| {3} 34°50.419'N; 111°48.956'W |
| {4} 34°50.566'N; 111°48.726'W |
| {5} 34°50.865'N; 111°48.818'W |
| {6} 34°51.187'N; 111°48.406'W |
| {7} 34°50.862'N; 111°48.117'W |
| {8} 34°50.732'N; 111°48.165'W |

Trail type	Loop
Challenge level	Moderate
Hiking distance (total)	5 miles
Cumulative ascent	675 feet

Pyramid Loop

Summary: A loop hike circling Sedona's Pyramid, which is visible from the end of the Tabletop Trail off the west side of the Airport Loop Trail

Challenge Level: Easy to Moderate

Hiking Distance: About 2.3 miles round trip

Hiking Time: About 1 ½ hours round trip

Trail Popularity:

Trailhead Directions: From the "Y" roundabout (see page 5), drive west on SR 89A about 4.25 miles then turn left onto the Upper Red Rock Loop Road. Sedona High School is on your right. Follow the Upper Red Rock Loop Road for 1.8 miles to the intersection of Chavez Ranch Road then park on the right side of the road {1}. There is room for about 12 vehicles here. You'll see the trail to the west from the parking area.

Description: This former mountain bike trail was opened in February 2016. The Pyramid Trail (combined with the Scorpion Trail) circles around the base of the Pyramid rock formation. You'll need good hiking boots with excellent traction because there are places where the trail is steep with loose gravel.

To hike the loop, you'll hike part of both the Scorpion and the Pyramid Trails. From the parking area, hike west for 300 feet to the signpost at the intersection of the Scorpion and the Pyramid Trail {2}. You'll come back here on the return trip. We suggest you hike the loop in the counterclockwise direction for the best views. So turn right then follow the Scorpion Trail. This trail gently rises for the next mile. You'll pass by a fence after 0.5 mile {3} and have a nice view behind you after 0.8 mile {4}. After 1 mile, you'll intersect the Pyramid Trail on your left at the signpost with large cairn {5}. Make a very sharp left turn here to follow the Pyramid Trail.

The Pyramid Trail is relatively flat for about the next 0.4 mile. You'll come to another nice view of Cathedral Rock {6} then begin a rather steep descent. There are excellent views all along this section of the trail. But the trail here is very narrow, with loose dirt and rocks as well as uneven in places with large drop offs so watch your footing. There's a nice place to stop for a snack just before you make a sharp right turn at about the 1.6 mile mark {7}. You'll have continuing views of Cathedral Rock on your way back to the intersection of the Pyramid and the Scorpion Trail {2}. When you arrive back, continue straight ahead to return to the parking area {1}.

Note: There is little shade on this trail so it is a good choice for cooler weather.

Color Photos: Scan the QR code for color photos of this trail

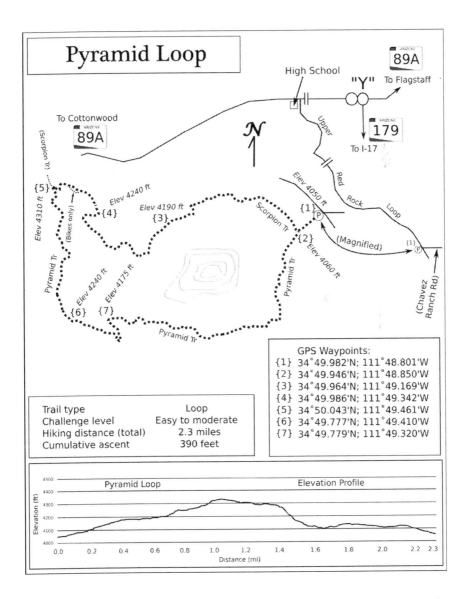

Rabbit Ears Trail

Summary: An in-out hike to a very distinct rock formation

Challenge Level: Moderate

Hiking Distance: About 2.5 miles each way from the Bell Rock Vista parking area or 5 miles round trip; about 1.4 miles each way from the Jacks Canyon parking area or 2.8 miles round trip

Hiking Time: About 2 ½ hours from the Bell Rock Vista parking area round trip; about 1 ½ hours from the Jacks Canyon Road parking area round trip

Trail Popularity:

Trailhead Directions: There are two trailheads for this trail: Bell Rock Vista and Jacks Canyon Road. From the "Y" roundabout (see page 5), proceed south on SR 179 about 6.25 miles. You'll pass the Court House Vista parking area on your left, just north of Bell Rock. Continue on SR 179 another 3/4 mile or so, you'll see another parking area on your left, south of Bell Rock. Turn left here into the Bell Rock Vista parking area {1}.

To reach the Jacks Canyon Road trailhead, continue south on SR 179, past the Bell Rock Vista parking area about 1 mile then turn left at the third roundabout onto Jacks Canyon Road. Watch for a sharp right turn after about 1 mile and continue on Jacks Canyon Road for a total of 2 miles. The parking area is up the access road on the right located across the road from Canyon Ridge Trail {2}.

Description: From the Bell Rock Vista parking area, hike past the interpretive signboard for 0.1 mile then turn right to go to the Big Park Loop Trail {3}. You'll intersect the Big Park Loop Trail in about 175 feet {4}. Turn right onto the Big Park Loop Trail. You'll intersect the Middle Trail after about 0.5 mile {5} and several unmarked trails as you hike east then north. After 1.3 miles, you'll see a large wash ahead. About 80 feet before you enter the wash, look for an unmarked trail on the right we call the Ridge Trail {6}. Turn right then begin climbing up. If you go into the wash, you've gone too far. As you hike east, the trail gently rises. You'll intersect the unnamed trail from the Jacks Canyon Road parking area after 1.1 miles {7}. Here, look north for a steep downward trail that takes you to the base of Rabbit Ears and an outstanding view {8}.

From the Jacks Canyon Road parking area, don't go through the gate for the Jacks Canyon Trail, but walk 25 paces to the northwest, back down the access road you drove in on. Find the unmarked trail to Rabbit Ears on the right. Go through each gate on both sides of Jacks Canyon Road. In 0.3 mile, you'll pass through a third gate {9}. Continue for another 1 mile. Watch for the intersection with the Ridge Trail {7} and the steep downward trail that leads to the view of Rabbit Ears {8}. There isn't much shade on either of the trails leading to Rabbit Ears so it is a hot hike in the summer.

Color Photos: Scan the QR code for color photos of this trail

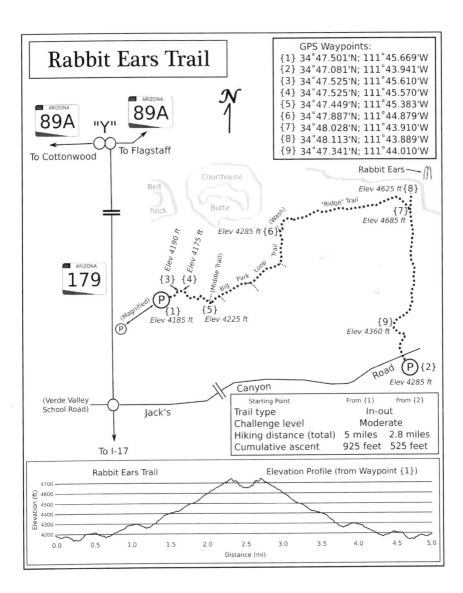

	Starting Point	From {1}	From {2}
Trail type		In-out	
Challenge level		Moderate	
Hiking distance (total)		5 miles	2.8 miles
Cumulative ascent		925 feet	525 feet

Schuerman Mountain Trail ★

Summary: An in-out hike up the side of a mountain with wonderful panoramic views of Cathedral Rock and other notable landmarks

Challenge Level: Moderate

Hiking Distance: About 0.5 mile to the top then another 0.25 miles to the southern overlook, and another 0.25 mile to the northern overlook or 2 miles round trip

Hiking Time: About 1 ½ hours round trip

Trail Popularity: 🚶🚶

Trailhead Directions: From the "Y" roundabout (see page 5), drive west toward Cottonwood on SR 89A about 4.25 miles. Turn left onto the Upper Red Rock Loop Road. Sedona High School is on your right. Turn right at the third driveway (it's behind the school) then look immediately for the sign to the trailhead parking area on the left {1}.

Description: Schuerman Mountain Trail provides great views of Cathedral Rock and other red rock views to the south. You begin by hiking behind the Red Rock High School where you'll intersect the Scorpion Trail on the left {2} then see a large array of solar panels as big as the school's football field capable of producing over 800 kilowatts of power (equivalent to powering 125 homes). After 0.2 mile, the trail goes around a gate, placed there when cattle once grazed the area. The trail up is steep in places, so watch your footing. If you hike in April, you may encounter wildflowers blooming. When you get to the top {3}, you'll see a Schuerman Mountain Trail sign pointing straight ahead (west). We don't recommend hiking this trail because the views are limited. Rather, take the trail to the left (south) for a good view of Cathedral Rock {4}. The best views of Cathedral Rock from the southern view point are in the afternoon. You can also take the faint (and unmarked) trail to the right to the top to look northwest toward the Verde Valley and Mingus Mountain {5}. Note that the trail up and on top of Schuerman Mountain is very rocky in places.

Color Photos: Scan the QR code for color photos of this trail

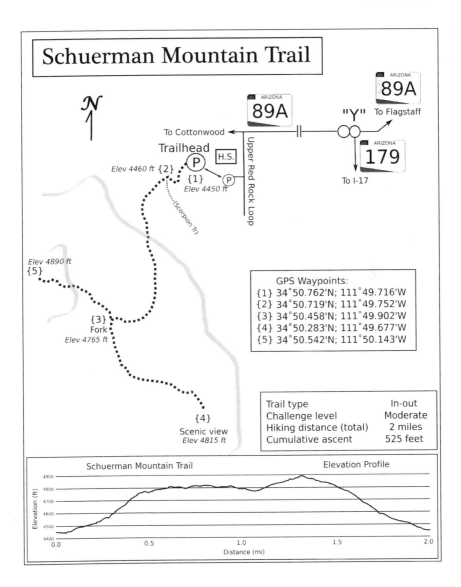

Schuerman Mountain Trail

To Cottonwood ←
Trailhead
Elev 4460 ft {2}
H.S.
{1}
Elev 4450 ft

Upper Red Rock Loop

(Scorpion Tr)

89A
89A
"Y" To Flagstaff
179
To I-17

To Flagstaff

Elev 4890 ft {5}

{3} Fork
Elev 4765 ft

{4}
Scenic view
Elev 4815 ft

GPS Waypoints:
{1} 34°50.762'N; 111°49.716'W
{2} 34°50.719'N; 111°49.752'W
{3} 34°50.458'N; 111°49.902'W
{4} 34°50.283'N; 111°49.677'W
{5} 34°50.542'N; 111°50.143'W

Trail type	In-out
Challenge level	Moderate
Hiking distance (total)	2 miles
Cumulative ascent	525 feet

Schuerman Mountain Trail — Elevation Profile

Scorpion Trail

Summary: An in-out hike around the northeast side of Sedona's Pyramid with great views of Cathedral Rock

Challenge Level: Moderate

Hiking Distance: About 2.1 miles each way or 4.2 miles round trip from the parking area behind the High School {1} to the parking area on the Upper Red Rock Loop Road {2} and return

Hiking Time: About 2 hours from the parking behind the High School to the parking on Red Rock Loop Road and return round trip

Trail Popularity:

Trailhead Directions: There are two trailheads you can use for this trail. From the "Y" roundabout (see page 5), drive west on SR 89A about 4.25 miles then turn left onto the Upper Red Rock Loop Road. Sedona High School is on your right. Turn right at the third driveway (it's behind the school) then look immediately for the sign to the trailhead parking area on the left for the Schuerman Mountain Trail {1}. To get to the second parking area, follow the Upper Red Rock Loop Road for 1.8 miles to the intersection of Chavez Ranch Road then park on the right side of the road {2}. You'll see the trail heading west from the parking area

Description: From the parking area behind the high school {1}, hike the Schuerman Mountain Trail for about 500 feet. Turn left (south) at the sign for the Scorpion Trail {3} located about 50 paces beyond the telephone pole. Follow this narrow, rocky former bike path. You'll have excellent views of the Pyramid and Cathedral Rock as you hike along. At 1.1 miles, you'll intersect the Pyramid Trail on the right {4} then come to a nice view of Cathedral Rock at 1.2 miles {5}. As you continue skirting the Pyramid, you'll pass through a fence {6} then come to the intersection with the other end of the Pyramid Trail {7}. The Pyramid Trail skirts the southern and western side of the Pyramid.

If you begin the hike from the second parking area on Red Rock Loop Road {2}, go west from the parking area for 350 feet to the signpost at the intersection of the Scorpion and the Pyramid Trail {7}. Make a right turn here to follow the Scorpion Trail.

Color Photos: Scan the QR code for color photos of this trail

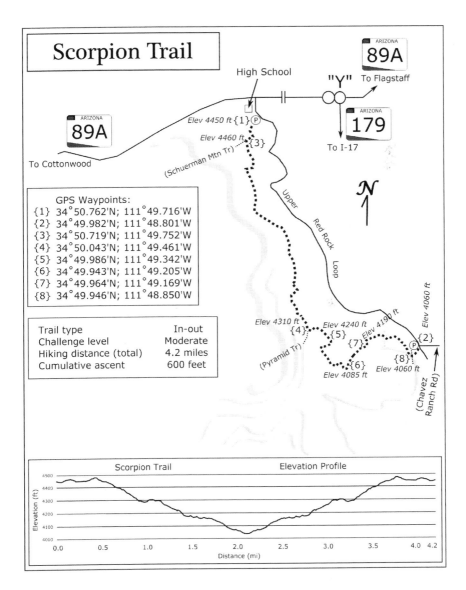

Secret Canyon Trail ★

Summary: A solitary in-out hike up a beautiful red rock canyon with the option for a loop hike

Challenge Level: Moderate to Hard

Hiking Distance: About 2.4 miles each way or 4.8 miles round trip

Hiking Time: About 2 ½ hours as an in-out hike round trip

Trail Popularity:

Trailhead Directions: From the "Y" roundabout (see page 5), drive west toward Cottonwood on SR 89A about 3 miles. Turn right onto Dry Creek Road (where speed limits are strictly enforced). Stay on Dry Creek Road for 2 miles then turn right onto Forest Road (FR) 152. Proceed on FR 152 for 3.4 miles to the parking area on your left {1}.

Note: FR 152 is an extremely rough road beyond the 0.2 mile paved section; a high clearance vehicle and 4WD are strongly recommended.

Description: We like this trail for its solitude. It is hard to get to (see description of FR 152 above) and in the Wilderness so there are no mountain bikers. The trail goes up a very picturesque canyon. You'll come to the HS Canyon Trail about 0.7 mile into the hike {2}. You'll cross a large wash at the 1.2 mile mark {3} and the David Miller Trail about 1.75 miles into the hike {4}.

If you wish to hike a loop, see Secret Canyon/Bear Sign Loop for directions on the 6.6 mile loop hike.

If you would rather hike in-out, continue on the Secret Canyon Trail. At about 2.4 miles, you'll be in a pine forest. Look to your left for a deep wash then follow the wash to the right for a short distance. If you are lucky, you may see a seasonal waterfall {5}. We usually stop after hiking 2.4 miles {5}, but the trail continues on another 2 miles, becoming steeper and rockier.

Color Photos: Scan the QR code for color photos of this trail

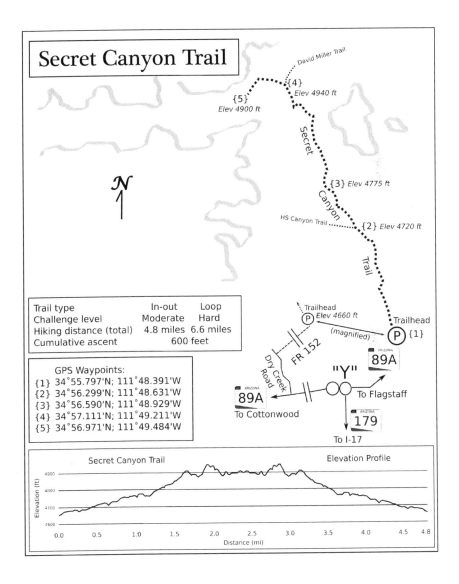

Secret Canyon Trail

David Miller Trail

{4} Elev 4940 ft

{5} Elev 4900 ft

Secret

{3} Elev 4775 ft

Canyon

HS Canyon Trail .... {2} Elev 4720 ft

Trail

Trail type	In-out	Loop
Challenge level	Moderate	Hard
Hiking distance (total)	4.8 miles	6.6 miles
Cumulative ascent	600 feet	

GPS Waypoints:
{1} 34°55.797'N; 111°48.391'W
{2} 34°56.299'N; 111°48.631'W
{3} 34°56.590'N; 111°48.929'W
{4} 34°57.111'N; 111°49.211'W
{5} 34°56.971'N; 111°49.484'W

Trailhead
(P) Elev 4660 ft
(magnified)

Trailhead
(P) {1}

FR 152

Dry Creek Road

ARIZONA
89A

"Y"

ARIZONA
89A ←
To Cottonwood

To Flagstaff

ARIZONA
179

To I-17

Secret Canyon Trail — Elevation Profile

Elevation (ft): 4900, 4800, 4700, 4600

Distance (mi): 0.0 0.5 1.0 1.5 2.0 2.5 3.0 3.5 4.0 4.5 4.8

Secret Canyon/Bear Sign Loop

Summary: A solitary loop hike through several beautiful red rock canyons

Challenge Level: Hard

Hiking Distance: 6.6 mile loop hike

Hiking Time: About 4 hours round trip

Trail Popularity: 🚶🚶

Trailhead Directions: From the "Y" roundabout (see page 5), drive west toward Cottonwood on SR 89A about 3 miles. Turn right onto Dry Creek Road (where speed limits are strictly enforced). Stay on Dry Creek Road for 2 miles then turn right onto Forest Road (FR) 152. Proceed on FR 152 for 3.4 miles to the Secret Canyon parking area on your left {1}.

Note: FR 152 is an extremely rough road beyond the 0.2 mile paved section; a high clearance vehicle and 4WD are strongly recommended.

Description: We like this trail for its solitude. It is hard to get to (see description of FR 152 above) and in the Wilderness so there are no mountain bikers. The trail goes up a very picturesque canyon. You'll come to the HS Canyon Trail about 0.7 mile into the hike {2}. You'll cross a large wash at the 1.2 mile mark {3}.

The David Miller Trail (named after a forest ranger who went missing in the area) appears after 1.75 miles {4}. Make a right turn here then begin a rather steep uphill climb then steep downhill for the next 0.6 mile. When you come to the Bear Sign Trail, make a right turn to begin the journey back {5}. Bear Sign crosses several washes and has the feeling of deep wilderness. After hiking Bear Sign for 2.2 miles, you'll intersect the Dry Creek Trail on your left {6}. Continue on Bear Sign for another 0.6 mile back to FR 152 {7}. Make a right onto FR 152 then walk down the road for about 1 mile to return to the Secret Canyon parking area {1}.

Color Photos: Scan the QR code for color photos of this trail

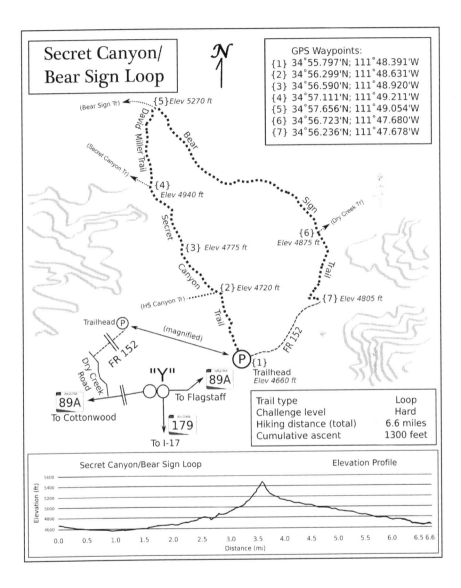

Secret Canyon/ Bear Sign Loop

GPS Waypoints:
{1} 34°55.797'N; 111°48.391'W
{2} 34°56.299'N; 111°48.631'W
{3} 34°56.590'N; 111°48.920'W
{4} 34°57.111'N; 111°49.211'W
{5} 34°57.656'N; 111°49.054'W
{6} 34°56.723'N; 111°47.680'W
{7} 34°56.236'N; 111°47.678'W

(Bear Sign Tr) {5} Elev 5270 ft

David Miller Trail

Bear

(Secret Canyon Tr) {4} Elev 4940 ft

Secret

Sign

(Dry Creek Tr)

{6} Elev 4875 ft

{3} Elev 4775 ft

Canyon

Trail

{2} Elev 4720 ft

{7} Elev 4805 ft

(HS Canyon Tr)

Trail

Trailhead (P)

(magnified)

FR 152

Dry Creek Road

FR 152

(P) {1}
Trailhead
Elev 4660 ft

"Y"

89A

To Flagstaff

89A

To Cottonwood

179

To I-17

Trail type	Loop
Challenge level	Hard
Hiking distance (total)	6.6 miles
Cumulative ascent	1300 feet

Secret Canyon/Bear Sign Loop — Elevation Profile

Elevation (ft): 5600, 5400, 5200, 5000, 4800, 4600

Distance (mi): 0.0, 0.5, 1.0, 1.5, 2.0, 2.5, 3.0, 3.5, 4.0, 4.5, 5.0, 5.5, 6.0, 6.5 6.6

Skywalker/Herkenham Loop

Summary: A loop hike on the western edge of Sedona featuring views of Cathedral Rock, Courthouse Butte and West Sedona

Challenge Level:
Moderate

Hiking Distance:
About 3.8 mile loop hike

Hiking Time:
About 2 ½ hours round trip

Trail Popularity:

Trailhead

Directions: From the "Y" roundabout (see page 5), drive west toward Cottonwood on SR 89A about 4.25 miles. Turn left onto the Upper Red Rock Loop Road. Sedona High School is on your right. Turn right at the third driveway (it's behind the school) then look immediately for the sign to the trailhead parking area on the left {1}. The trail begins across Upper Red Rock Loop Road {2}.

Description: You'll be hiking three trails to complete the loop which are Skywalker, Old Post and Herkenham trails. Skywalker and Herkenham are narrow with ups and downs while Old Post is a gentle downhill hike. An afternoon hike will give you excellent views to the south.

Begin by hiking Skywalker. In 0.2 mile, you'll intersect the Over Easy Trail, which is a little loop trail. You'll intersect it again after 0.5 mile. At 0.7 mile, you'll come to a bench with nice views to the south {3}. Just beyond the bench the trail becomes very narrow with a large drop off for 0.2 mile so watch your footing.

You'll see houses all along the Skywalker Trail but they really don't distract from the pleasant views. At 1.1 miles, you'll come to the highest point on the trail {4} and have a nice view of West Sedona to the north. At 1.3 miles, you'll be under a power line {5}, then in 2 miles you'll intersect the Old Post Trail {6}. Make a right turn here onto the Old Post Trail but look north here for a nice view of Thunder Mountain.

After 0.5 mile, you'll intersect the Carroll Canyon Trail on the left {7}. Continue on the Old Post Trail. You'll intersect the Herkenham Trail at 2.9 miles {8}. Turn right here then begin a series of ups and downs as you head northwest. At 3.3

miles, the trail turns left at the bottom of a wash {9}. Continue on Herkenham back to the trailhead {2}.

Color Photos: Scan the QR code for color photos of this trail

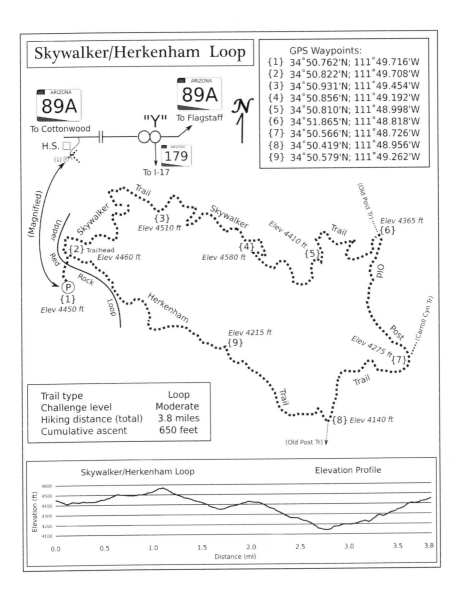

Slim Shady/Hermit Loop

Summary: A partially shaded loop hike using several popular mountain biking trails with nice red rock views

Challenge Level: Easy

Hiking Distance: About 2.7 miles loop

Hiking Time: About 2 hours round trip

Trail Popularity:

Trailhead Directions: From the "Y" roundabout (see page 5), drive south on SR 179 about 4.8 miles to mile marker 308.5 then turn right into the Yavapai Vista parking area {1}.

Note: The parking area is accessible only from southbound SR 179. The trail begins on the southwest side of the parking area.

Description: There are a number of short, interconnected trails here but we prefer to hike the short loop hike described below in the clockwise direction. An afternoon hike will produce the best photos. Just past the interpretive signboard, turn left onto an unmarked trail. (If you continue straight ahead, you will come to the intersection of the Kaibab and Yavapai Vista Trails {2}.) Follow the short connector trail for about 200 feet until you intersect the Coconino Trail {3}. Turn right then follow the Coconino Trail for 0.3 mile then make a right turn onto the Slim Shady Trail {4}. You'll come to the intersection with the HiLine Trail on the left after 0.1 mile and the Kaibab Trail on the right after 0.2 mile {5}. Continue on the Slim Shady Trail. You'll soon be in a wash which provides shade in the summer for the next 0.2 mile. Look to the right for good views of Lee Mountain, the Two Nuns and Rabbit Ears. At 1.1 miles from the parking area, you'll come to an open bluff that makes a nice snack spot {6}.

After 1.7 miles from the parking area, you'll come to the intersection of the Templeton and HT Trails {7}. Make a right then follow the Templeton Trail. You'll see a "social trail" on your right after 0.1 mile – continue straight ahead. After another 0.3 mile, you'll intersect the Easy Breezy Trail on the left {8}. Continue on the Templeton Trail for another 0.2 mile to the intersection with the Hermit Trail {9}. Turn right then follow the Hermit Trail for 0.4 mile back to the parking area.

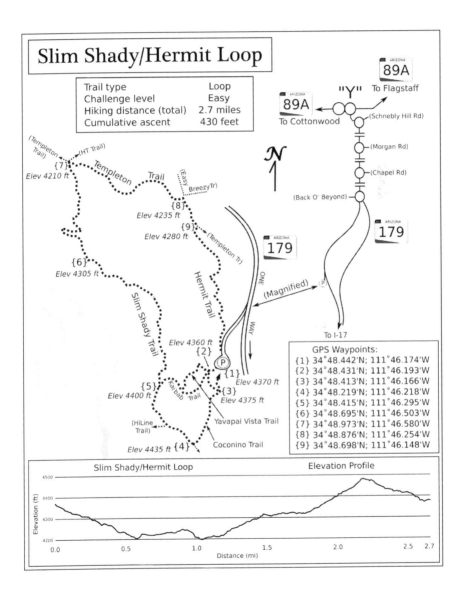

Slim Shady/Hermit Loop

Trail type	Loop
Challenge level	Easy
Hiking distance (total)	2.7 miles
Cumulative ascent	430 feet

ARIZONA
89A

"Y" To Flagstaff

ARIZONA
89A

To Cottonwood
(Schnebly Hill Rd)

(Morgan Rd)

(Chapel Rd)

(Back O' Beyond)

ARIZONA
179

(Templeton Trail)
(HT Trail)
{7}
Elev 4210 ft
Templeton Trail
(Easy Breezy Tr)

{8}
Elev 4235 ft
{9}
Elev 4280 ft
(Templeton Tr)

ARIZONA
179

(Magnified)
P

N

{6}
Elev 4305 ft

Slim Shady Trail

Hermit Trail

ONE WAY

To I-17

Elev 4360 ft
{2}
P
{1}
Elev 4370 ft

Kaibab Trail

{5}
Elev 4400 ft
{3}
Elev 4375 ft

(HiLine Trail)
Yavapai Vista Trail

Elev 4435 ft {4}
Coconino Trail

GPS Waypoints:
{1} 34°48.442'N; 111°46.174'W
{2} 34°48.431'N; 111°46.193'W
{3} 34°48.413'N; 111°46.166'W
{4} 34°48.219'N; 111°46.218'W
{5} 34°48.415'N; 111°46.295'W
{6} 34°48.695'N; 111°46.503'W
{7} 34°48.973'N; 111°46.580'W
{8} 34°48.876'N; 111°46.254'W
{9} 34°48.698'N; 111°46.148'W

Slim Shady/Hermit Loop   Elevation Profile

Elevation (ft)

4500
4400
4300
4200

0.0   0.5   1.0   1.5   2.0   2.5 2.7
Distance (mi)

Soldier Pass Trail ★

Summary: An in-out hike with stops at the Devil's Kitchen and the Seven Sacred Pools along with a side trip to some impressive red rock arches and the option for a loop hike

Challenge Level: Moderate

Hiking Distance: About 2.1 miles one way to the Brins Mesa Trail or 4.2 miles round trip

Hiking Time: About 3 hours round trip

Trail Popularity:

Trailhead Directions: From the "Y" roundabout (see page 5), drive west toward Cottonwood on SR 89A for 1.25 miles then turn right onto Soldiers Pass Road. Proceed on Soldiers Pass for 1.5 miles. Turn right onto Rim Shadows. Go approximately 0.25 mile then turn left into the parking area {1}. The gate to the parking area is open from 8:00 am to 6:00 pm. If you get back to your car after 6:00 pm, you won't be able to drive out of the parking area. There is room for only about 12 vehicles here so try to come early or you may have to wait for a parking spot. There is no parking on adjacent streets.

Description: Shortly after beginning the Soldier Pass Trail, you'll descend into the deep Soldier Wash then climb up to the Devil's Kitchen (about 0.2 mile) {2}. This is the largest sinkhole in the Sedona area. After another 0.4 mile, you'll come to the Seven Sacred Pools, which are small depressions in the red rock that hold water even in dry periods {3}. These two areas are very popular with visitors on jeep rides and hikers. You won't encounter jeeps or as many other hikers on the rest of the trail. There is partial shade beginning at about the 1 mile mark and the trees tend to block some of the red rock views.

About 1.3 miles from the trailhead, look to the right for a faint trail up to the Soldier Pass Arches {4}. It's a steep climb of about 275 feet with drop offs so be extremely careful if you attempt to go to the arches. Return to the main trail. As you continue, the trail becomes rockier and steeper as it climbs up to Brins Mesa. Once on top of Brins Mesa, you'll come to a fork at the 2 mile mark {6}. Take the right fork to an overlook {8} or take the left fork to the intersection with the Brins Mesa Trail after another 0.1 mile {7}.

Turn around here, or you can hike a loop by turning right onto the Brins Mesa Trail (see Brins Mesa/Soldier Pass Loop).

Color Photos: Scan the QR code for color photos of this trail

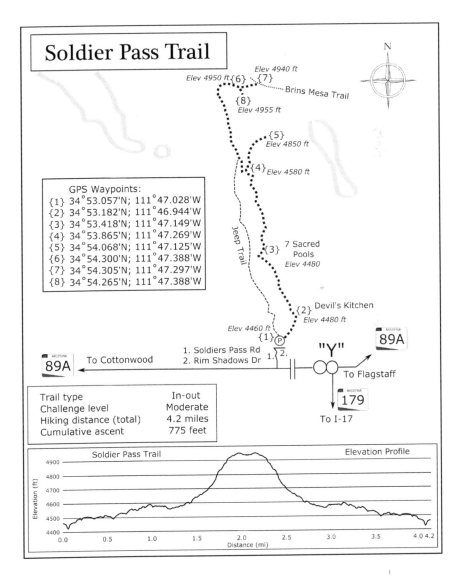

Soldier Pass Trail

N

Elev 4940 ft

Elev 4950 ft {6} ··{7}
·········· Brins Mesa Trail

{8}
Elev 4955 ft

{5}
Elev 4850 ft

{4} Elev 4580 ft

GPS Waypoints:
{1} 34°53.057'N; 111°47.028'W
{2} 34°53.182'N; 111°46.944'W
{3} 34°53.418'N; 111°47.149'W
{4} 34°53.865'N; 111°47.269'W
{5} 34°54.068'N; 111°47.125'W
{6} 34°54.300'N; 111°47.388'W
{7} 34°54.305'N; 111°47.297'W
{8} 34°54.265'N; 111°47.388'W

Jeep Trail

{3} 7 Sacred Pools
Elev 4480

{2} Devil's Kitchen
Elev 4480 ft

Elev 4460 ft
{1} P

1. Soldiers Pass Rd
2. Rim Shadows Dr

1. 2.

"Y"

ARIZONA 89A

ARIZONA 89A

To Cottonwood

To Flagstaff

ARIZONA 179

To I-17

Trail type	In-out
Challenge level	Moderate
Hiking distance (total)	4.2 miles
Cumulative ascent	775 feet

Soldier Pass Trail

Elevation Profile

Elevation (ft)

4900

4800

4700

4600

4500

4400

0.0   0.5   1.0   1.5   2.0   2.5   3.0   3.5   4.0 4.2

Distance (mi)

Soldier Wash Trails
Adobe Jack/Javelina Loop

Summary: A loop hike that offers a short detour to a beautiful overlook with wonderful views

Challenge Level:
Moderate

Hiking Distance:
About a 4.6 mile loop (including the side trip to the top of Ant Hill)

Hiking Time:
About 2 ½ hours as a loop hike round trip

Trail Popularity:

Trailhead

Directions: From the "Y" roundabout (see page 5), drive towards Cottonwood 0.8 mile then turn right into the small parking area along SR 89A. There are only 5 parking spaces here but you can squeeze in 2 more vehicles {1}.

Description: There are seven connecting trails within the Soldier Wash Trail System, which were mountain bike trails adopted by the Forest Service. This is a loop by hiking up the western side of the system on the Adobe Jack Trail, stopping at a beautiful overlook then continuing back on the east side via the Javelina Trail. The views improve the further north you hike.

From the parking area, follow the signs for the Adobe Jack Trail. After 350 feet, you descend into a large wash, then intersect the Crusty Trail {2}. You'll be returning via the Crusty Trail. For now, continue on Adobe Jack. Throughout this hike all of the trails rise and fall. You'll intersect the Coyote Trail {3} after 0.8 mile then the Power Line Plunge Trail after 1 mile {4}. Make a right turn onto Power Line Plunge.

As you hike Power Line Plunge, you'll intersect the Manzanita Trail {5} and Shorty Trail{6}. After 1.4 miles, you'll intersect the Grand Central Trail {7}. Here we suggest you make a left then follow the Grand Central Trail for 0.6 mile to the top of Ant Hill {10} for fantastic views. You'll pass the Shorty Trail {8}and the Ant Hill Loop {9} on the way. The Grand Central Trail rises gently between {7} and {9} but is very steep between {9} and {10} so watch your footing.

Once you've enjoyed the views from the top of Ant Hill, return to the Power Line Plunge Trail then make a left turn to continue on. At 2.75 miles, continue across an open area {11}. At 2.8 miles, you'll intersect the Javelina Trail {12}.

Make a right turn here to begin the hike back. You"ll intersect the Manzanita Trail again at 3.4 miles {13} and the Grand Central Trail again at 4 miles {14}. Continue west on the Grand Central Trail. You'll be following a large wash parallel with SR 89A. You'll intersect the end of the Crusty Trail at 4.2 miles {15}. Continue west on the Crusty Trail for another 0.5 mile to the intersection of the Crusty Trail and Adobe Jack {2}. Make a left turn here and follow Adobe Jack a short distance back to the parking area {1} for a 4.6 mile loop hike.

Color Photos: Scan the QR code for color photos of this trail

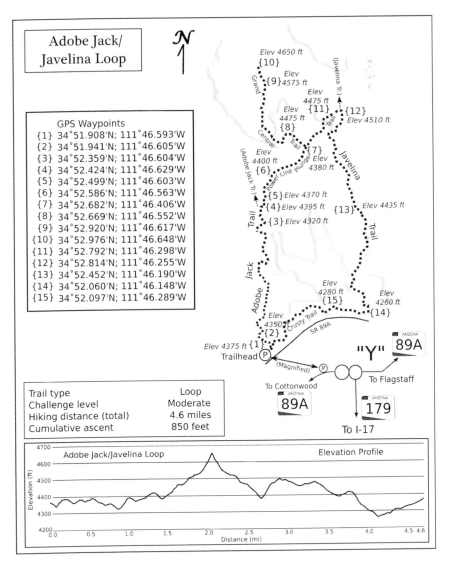

123

Soldier Wash Trails
Grand Central/Javelina Loop

Summary: A loop hike that passes a beautiful overlook with wonderful views

Challenge Level: Moderate

Hiking Distance: About a 5 mile loop

Hiking Time: About 2 ½ hours as a loop hike round trip

Trail Popularity: 🚶🚶 🚶🚶

Trailhead Directions: From the "Y" roundabout (see page 5), drive towards Cottonwood 0.8 mile then turn right into the small parking area along SR 89A. There are only 5 parking spaces here but you can squeeze in 2 more vehicles

Description: There are seven connecting trails within the Soldier Wash Trail System, which were mountain bike trails adopted by the Forest Service. This is a loop by hiking up the center of the system on the Grand Central Trail, stopping at a beautiful overlook then continuing back on the east side via the Javelina Trail. The views improve the further north you hike.

From the parking area, follow the signs for the Adobe Jack Trail. After 350 feet, you descend into a large wash then hike up to make a sharp right turn onto the Crusty Trail. As you proceed, you cross back and forth and hike in the wash for a large part of the way. After 0.6 mile, you'll intersect the Grand Central Trail (GCT) {2}. Make a left turn then begin hiking north for 1.4 miles. The GCT is very shaded for the first 0.5 mile. As you hike along, you'll intersect the Coyote, Power Line Plunge and Shorty Trails. When you intersect the Ant Hill Loop Trail, turn left; walk 7 paces then turn right to continue on the GCT. The trail now becomes steep and there is loose rock so watch your footing. After 0.1 mile, look to the left for a high red rock knoll known as Ant Hill which is a great place to stop for photos and a snack {3}. You'll have 360 degree views and can see Bell Rock, Courthouse Butte, Sugarloaf, Chimney Rock, Snoopy, Lucy and other Sedona landmarks. If you like, this is a good place to turn around and return to the parking area for a 4 mile round trip hike.

However, if you want to hike a loop, continue north on the GCT for 0.3 mile then make a right turn onto the Ant Hill Loop Trail {4}. Follow the Ant Hill Loop Trail for 0.2 mile then make a right turn (east) onto the Jordan Trail {5}.

Follow the Jordan Trail for 0.5 mile then turn right (south) onto the Javelina Trail {6}. Follow the Javelina Trail for 1.2 miles then turn right (west) onto the GCT {7}. Follow the GCT for 0.1 mile then continue on the Crusty Trail {2} for 0.6 mile back to the parking area {1}.

Color Photos: Scan the QR code for color photos of this trail

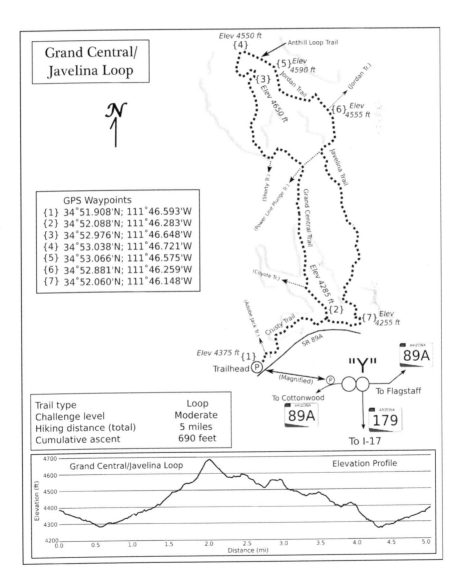

Sterling Pass to Vultee Arch Trails

Summary: An in-out hike up the west side of Oak Creek Canyon and an alternative way to hike to Vultee Arch

Challenge Level:
Hard

Hiking Distance:
About 4.5 miles from the Sterling Pass parking area to the Vultee Arch parking area located at the end of Forest Road 152 {4}; about 2.6 miles each way from Sterling Pass trailhead to Vultee Arch or 5.2 miles round trip

Hiking Time: About 3 ½ hours to Vultee Arch and return round trip

Trail Popularity:

Trailhead
Directions: From the "Y" roundabout (see page 5), drive north on SR 89A about 6.25 miles. You'll need to find a wide spot in the road to park on the west side near mile marker 380.5, about 300 feet north of the Manzanita campground located on the east side of SR 89A. The trail starts on the west side of SR 89A {1}.

Description: You can reach Vultee Arch {5} from the Sterling Pass Trail. Sterling Pass is very steep with areas you have to climb up, has loose rock in places and can be overgrown but is easy to follow. Watch for poison ivy along the trail.

You'll hike up about 1150 feet to reach the saddle {2}. The saddle is about 1.4 miles from the SR 89A parking area. As you continue from the saddle, you'll enter a pine forest and the trail begins a steady descent.

About 2.4 miles in, you've reached the end of the Sterling Pass Trail and you'll see a sign for Vultee Arch on the right {3}. Turn right here then hike 0.2 mile down the Vultee Arch Trail to see Vultee Arch, an impressive sight {5} (see Vultee Arch Trail).

Color Photos: Scan the QR code for color photos of this trail

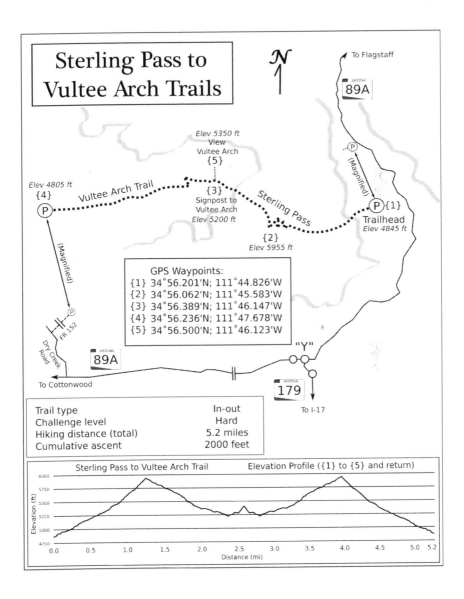

Sterling Pass to Vultee Arch Trails

N

To Flagstaff

89A

Elev 5350 ft
View
Vultee Arch
{5}

Elev 4805 ft
{4}
Vultee Arch Trail
P

{3}
Signpost to
Vultee Arch
Elev 5200 ft

Sterling Pass

P {1}
Trailhead
Elev 4845 ft

{2}
Elev 5955 ft

(Magnified)

P
FR 152

Dry Creek Road

89A

To Cottonwood

GPS Waypoints:
{1} 34°56.201'N; 111°44.826'W
{2} 34°56.062'N; 111°45.583'W
{3} 34°56.389'N; 111°46.147'W
{4} 34°56.236'N; 111°47.678'W
{5} 34°56.500'N; 111°46.123'W

"Y"

179

To I-17

Trail type	In-out
Challenge level	Hard
Hiking distance (total)	5.2 miles
Cumulative ascent	2000 feet

Sterling Pass to Vultee Arch Trail   Elevation Profile ({1} to {5} and return)

Elevation (ft)

6000
5750
5500
5250
5000
4750

0.0   0.5   1.0   1.5   2.0   2.5   3.0   3.5   4.0   4.5   5.0 5.2
Distance (mi)

Sugarloaf Trail

Summary: A short hike to a large rock mound with nice views of Capital Butte, Coffeepot and Sedona

Challenge Level: Moderate

Hiking Distance: About 2 miles loop

Hiking Time: About 1 hour round trip

Trail Popularity:

Trailhead Directions: From the "Y" roundabout (see page 5), drive west toward Cottonwood on SR 89A for just under 2 miles then turn right onto Coffeepot Drive. Drive about 0.5 mile then turn left at the stop sign onto Sanborn. Continue to the second street then turn right onto Little Elf. Little Elf ends at Buena Vista so make a short right onto Buena Vista then a quick left into the parking area {1}. This is the same parking area as the Coffeepot Trail. It has only 14 spots so can fill quickly.

Description: About 50 feet past the interpretive signboard near the parking area, look for a sign on the right {2}. Follow the Teacup/Sugarloaf Summit Trail for 0.3 mile. There are many "social trails" in this area so be sure to follow the cairns. Turn right at the next sign {3} then continue on the Teacup Trail. You'll soon come to a sign for the western end of the Sugarloaf Summit Loop Trail {4}. Continue straight ahead on the Teacup Trail for another 0.1 mile and you'll intersect an unmarked trail on your left that will lead you to the base of Coffeepot Rock {5} (see Coffeepot Trail). About 0.1 mile further on, turn right onto the Sugarloaf Summit Trail {6} at a trail marker where you'll have a nice view of Coffeepot Rock. Hike south then turn west under a power line. After 0.4 mile, you'll see a post on the right, opposite of where the trail to Sugarloaf Summit begins on your left {7}. After climbing to the summit (a scramble of some 0.2 mile that gains 200 feet in elevation) {8}, return to the Sugarloaf Loop Trail. Turn left (west) then continue on for another 0.1 mile. Turn left onto the Teacup Trail {4} then hike back to the parking area.

While you'll see rooftops on this in-town trail, the views of Capital Butte (also known as Thunder Mountain) and Coffeepot Rock are beautiful. There is little shade, however, so the hike would be hot in the summer months.

Color Photos: Scan the QR code for color photos of this trail

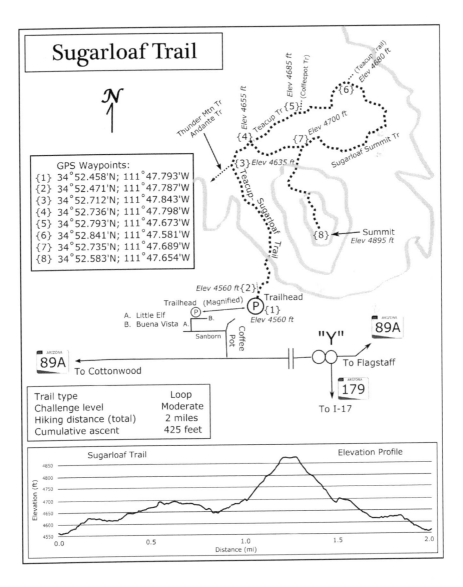

Sugarloaf Trail

N

GPS Waypoints:
{1} 34°52.458'N; 111°47.793'W
{2} 34°52.471'N; 111°47.787'W
{3} 34°52.712'N; 111°47.843'W
{4} 34°52.736'N; 111°47.798'W
{5} 34°52.793'N; 111°47.673'W
{6} 34°52.841'N; 111°47.581'W
{7} 34°52.735'N; 111°47.689'W
{8} 34°52.583'N; 111°47.654'W

Thunder Mtn Tr
Andante Tr

Elev 4655 ft
Teacup Tr {5}
Teacup Tr
Elev 4685 ft
(Coffeepot Tr)
{4}
{3} Elev 4635 ft
(Teacup Trail)
Elev 4680 ft
{6}
Elev 4700 ft
{7}
Sugarloaf Summit Tr

Teacup — Sugarloaf Trail

Sugarloaf Trail

{8}
Summit
Elev 4895 ft

Elev 4560 ft {2}
Trailhead (Magnified)
P
Trailhead
{1}
Elev 4560 ft

A. Little Elf
B. Buena Vista

P
B.
A.
Sanborn
Coffee Pot

"Y"

ARIZONA
89A

ARIZONA
89A
To Cottonwood

To Flagstaff

ARIZONA
179
To I-17

Trail type	Loop
Challenge level	Moderate
Hiking distance (total)	2 miles
Cumulative ascent	425 feet

Sugarloaf Trail — Elevation Profile

Elevation (ft)
4850
4800
4750
4700
4650
4600
4550
0.0   0.5   1.0   1.5   2.0
Distance (mi)

Telephone Trail

Summary: A short but steep hike up the east side of Oak Creek Canyon leading to amazing window rock formations

Challenge Level: Hard

Hiking Distance: About 1.3 miles each way or 2.6 miles round trip

Hiking Time: About 2 hours round trip

Trail Popularity: 🚶‍♂️

Trailhead Directions: From the "Y" roundabout (see page 5), drive north on SR 89A about 10.9 miles to mile post 385.1. Park on the east side of SR 89A on the paved shoulder beneath a 25 foot high cliff. The parking area {1} is 0.4 mile north of the turn to the West Fork parking area. Walk north along SR 89A for 475 feet to the trail sign on your right {2}. There you'll see a dark rust color sign for the Telephone Trail.

Description: The trail begins by following SR 89A under a telephone line (hence the name of the trail). After 0.3 mile, you'll begin a series of steep ascents up to several nice ridges {3}. Along the way there are some very nice rock formations and scenic views of Oak Creek Canyon. At 0.6 mile and a rather steep descent, you'll come to a series of unique window or keyhole rocks {4}. This would be a good place to have a snack, take some photos then turn back if you don't want to continue on the very steep trail ahead.

If you continue on, the trail becomes very steep with loose sand, rock and pine needles {5} {6}. The trail ends when you reach the top of the east wall of Oak Creek Canyon {7} but you can bushwhack about 1.6 miles to the north and intersect the Harding Springs Trail. For this endeavor, we recommend you use a GPS unit.

Note: The trail is very steep in places with loose sand and rock; do not attempt if the trail is wet or snow is present.

Color Photos: Scan the QR code for color photos of this trail

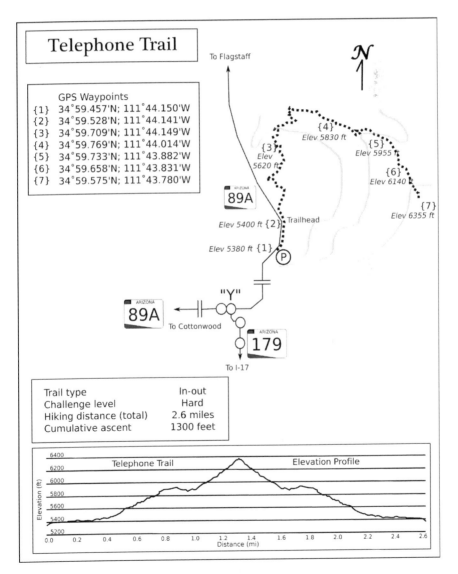

Telephone Trail

GPS Waypoints
{1} 34°59.457'N; 111°44.150'W
{2} 34°59.528'N; 111°44.141'W
{3} 34°59.709'N; 111°44.149'W
{4} 34°59.769'N; 111°44.014'W
{5} 34°59.733'N; 111°43.882'W
{6} 34°59.658'N; 111°43.831'W
{7} 34°59.575'N; 111°43.780'W

To Flagstaff

N

{4} Elev 5830 ft
{5} Elev 5955 ft
{3} Elev 5620 ft
{6} Elev 6140 ft

89A

Elev 5400 ft {2} Trailhead
Elev 5380 ft {1}
P

{7} Elev 6355 ft

"Y"

89A
To Cottonwood

179
To I-17

Trail type	In-out
Challenge level	Hard
Hiking distance (total)	2.6 miles
Cumulative ascent	1300 feet

Telephone Trail — Elevation Profile

Elevation (ft)
6400
6200
6000
5800
5600
5400
5200

Distance (mi)
0.0 0.2 0.4 0.6 0.8 1.0 1.2 1.4 1.6 1.8 2.0 2.2 2.4 2.6

Templeton Trail

Summary: A two-vehicle pass-the-key or in-out hike with views of Sedona's major rock formations

Challenge Level: Moderate

Hiking Distance: About 4.6 miles from the Court House Vista parking area to the Baldwin Loop Trail parking area; about 9.2 miles in-out

Hiking Time: About 2 ½ hours as a pass-the-key hike; about 5 hours as an in-out hike from the Court House Vista parking area to the Baldwin Loop Trail parking area and return

Trail Popularity: 🚶🚶🚶

Trailhead Directions: Park one vehicle at the Court House Vista parking area {1} (see Bell Rock Climb and Bell Rock Vortex) and one vehicle at the Baldwin Loop parking area {7} (see Baldwin Loop).

Description: The Templeton Trail extends northwest from the Bell Rock Pathway, just north of Bell Rock and Courthouse Butte to the Baldwin Loop trail near Oak Creek and Red Rock Crossing. It provides excellent views of Bell Rock, Courthouse Butte, Lee Mountain, Cathedral Rock and many other rock formations. There are several ways to hike this trail. You can do this trail as a pass-the-key two-vehicle hike (i.e. two groups hiking toward each other from the two separate trailheads and exchanging their vehicle keys). If you hike from the Court House Vista parking area, look for the Phone Trail on your left about 25 feet past the interpretive signboard {2}. Follow the Phone Trail 0.3 mile then continue north (left) on the Bell Rock Pathway Trail. In 0.1 mile turn left onto the Templeton Trail {3} then follow it beneath both the northbound and southbound lanes of SR 179. You'll have excellent views of Cathedral Rock ahead and, in 1 mile, you'll intersect the HT Trail on your right {4}. As you approach Cathedral Rock, the landscape becomes high desert.

You'll intersect the Cathedral Rock Trail in another 1.3 miles on your right {5} and the short but steep trail to the saddle of Cathedral Rock in another 200 feet on your left. As you continue on the Templeton Trail, you'll descend a series of switchbacks. In 0.8 mile, you'll be adjacent to Oak Creek, across from Buddha

132

Beach and Red Rock Crossing. The Templeton Trail continues on for another 0.2 mile where it ends at the Baldwin Loop trail {6}. Continue straight ahead on the Baldwin Loop trail for another 0.5 mile to the Baldwin Loop trail parking area on Verde Valley School Road {7} for a hike of 4.6 miles.

Color Photos: Scan the QR code for color photos of this trail

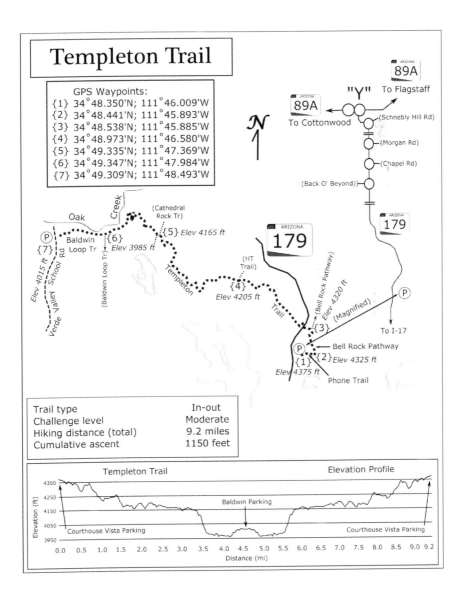

Templeton Trail

GPS Waypoints:
{1} 34°48.350'N; 111°46.009'W
{2} 34°48.441'N; 111°45.893'W
{3} 34°48.538'N; 111°45.885'W
{4} 34°48.973'N; 111°46.580'W
{5} 34°49.335'N; 111°47.369'W
{6} 34°49.347'N; 111°47.984'W
{7} 34°49.309'N; 111°48.493'W

Trail type	In-out
Challenge level	Moderate
Hiking distance (total)	9.2 miles
Cumulative ascent	1150 feet

Templeton Trail — Elevation Profile

Vultee Arch Trail

Summary: A shady in-out hike to a natural red rock arch

Challenge Level:
Easy to Moderate

Hiking Distance:
About 1.9 miles each way to view the arch, add another 0.3 mile to climb up on the arch or 3.8 miles round trip

Hiking Time:
About 2 hours round trip

Trail Popularity: 🚶

Trailhead Directions: From the "Y" roundabout (see page 5), drive west toward Cottonwood on SR 89A about 3 miles. Turn right onto Dry Creek Road (where speed limits are strictly enforced). Stay on Dry Creek Road for 2 miles then turn right onto Forest Road (FR) 152. Proceed to the end of FR 152 (about 4.5 miles) to the parking area on the left {1}.The parking area is the same as used for the Bear Sign and Dry Creek Trails. The Vultee Arch Trail begins on the east side of the parking area, on the right side of the interpretive signboard.

Note: FR 152 is an extremely rough road beyond the 0.2 mile paved section; a high clearance vehicle and 4WD are strongly recommended.

Description: The trail to the arch viewpoint is a relatively easy hike, but it is a scramble (thus the moderate trail rating) to get onto the arch {6} so be careful if you attempt this. The trail isn't used much because of the difficult drive to the trailhead, as a result this shaded trail can be overgrown. Even though it can be overgrown, it is easy to follow. Watch for poison ivy in some of the wash crossings {2} {3}.

The trail forks at a signpost {4} after about 1.5 miles. Follow the left fork to see the arch. The right fork becomes the Sterling Pass Trail which proceeds to SR 89A in Oak Creek Canyon (see Sterling Pass to Vultee Arch Trails). The arch is visible to the north from the view area {5}. Vultee Arch is named after Gerald and Sylvia Vultee who crashed their plane and died nearby in 1938. There is a plaque dedicated to them near the view area for the arch. There are many wildflowers along the trail in late April/early May.

Note: The Forest Service reports that the arch is unstable so proceed onto the arch at your own risk.

Color Photos: Scan the QR code for color photos of this trail

Note: See Sterling Pass to Vultee Arch Trails for an alternate way to get to Vultee Arch

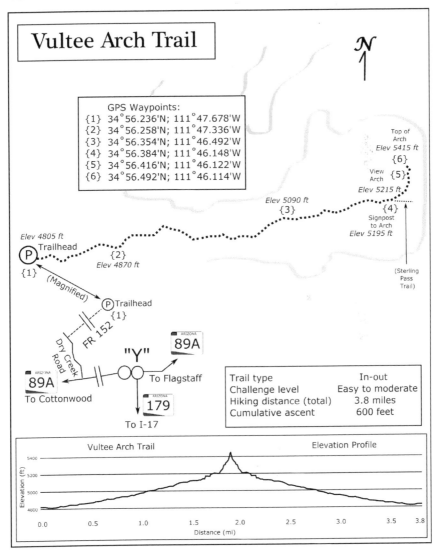

Vultee Arch Trail

N

GPS Waypoints:
{1} 34°56.236'N; 111°47.678'W
{2} 34°56.258'N; 111°47.336'W
{3} 34°56.354'N; 111°46.492'W
{4} 34°56.384'N; 111°46.148'W
{5} 34°56.416'N; 111°46.122'W
{6} 34°56.492'N; 111°46.114'W

Top of Arch
Elev 5415 ft
{6}
View Arch {5}
Elev 5215 ft

Elev 5090 ft
{3}
{4}
Signpost to Arch
Elev 5195 ft

Elev 4805 ft
Trailhead
(P)
{1}
(Magnified)
{2}
Elev 4870 ft

(Sterling Pass Trail)

(P) Trailhead
{1}

FR 152

Dry Creek Road

"Y"

ARIZONA 89A

89A ARIZONA
To Cottonwood

To Flagstaff

ARIZONA 179
To I-17

Trail type	In-out
Challenge level	Easy to moderate
Hiking distance (total)	3.8 miles
Cumulative ascent	600 feet

Vultee Arch Trail — Elevation Profile

Elevation (ft): 5400, 5200, 5000, 4800
Distance (mi): 0.0, 0.5, 1.0, 1.5, 2.0, 2.5, 3.0, 3.5, 3.8

West Fork Trail ★

Summary: A beautiful, shady in-out hike along the West Fork of Oak Creek

Challenge Level: Moderate

Hiking Distance: About 3.6 miles each way or 7.2 miles round trip

Hiking Time: About 4 hours round trip

Trail Popularity:

Trailhead Directions: From the "Y" roundabout (see page 5), drive north on SR 89A about 10.5 miles. Turn left into the parking area {1}. The trail starts on the far side of the parking area, furthest away from the entrance. There are toilets at the parking area. The gate to the parking area opens at 8:00 am. Use a prepay envelope if the parking attendant isn't on duty. It is a special fee area (see Required Parking Pass, page 145). The parking area fills quickly so arrive early in the morning.

Description: West Fork is considered by many to be the most beautiful trail in the Sedona area. You'll be crossing the water 13 times as you hike the trail. You have to step from stone to stone to cross, so the trail isn't recommended in high water times (you'll get your feet wet!!). After 0.3 mile you'll come to the remains of Mayhew's Lodge, built in the 1880s. It was remodeled in 1895 then burned down in 1980 {2}.

At the 0.4 mile mark, you'll come to the first of the 13 creek crossings {3}. As you continue along, look to the sides for some amazing red rock bluffs. There is a nice spot to stop after 1.1 miles {4}. Just across the 7th creek crossing is a natural stone bench which is another nice place to stop and rest. At 2.8 miles, you'll come to a huge overhang where the water has eroded the rock {5}. Continue another 0.4 mile and watch for a short side trail to a cave on your left {6}. At 3.6 miles, you'll effectively come to the end of the trail because you'll have to wade through the water to continue {7}.

West Fork has two wonderful seasons, spring and fall. The most beautiful is fall, when the deciduous trees display glorious colors. The third week in October seems to be when the colors are usually at their peak.

Color Photos: Scan the QR code for color photos of this trail

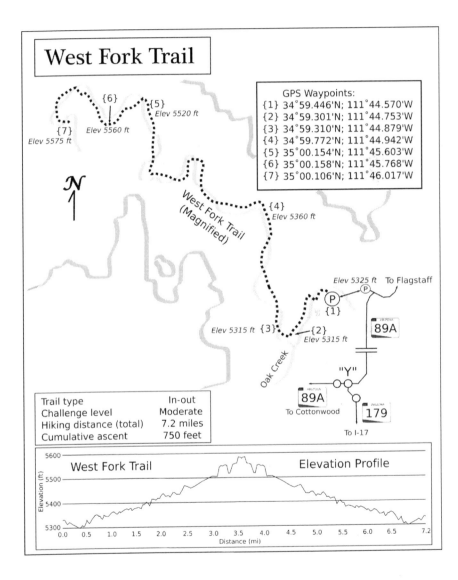

West Fork Trail

{6}

{5}
Elev 5520 ft

{7}
Elev 5575 ft

Elev 5560 ft

GPS Waypoints:
{1} 34°59.446'N; 111°44.570'W
{2} 34°59.301'N; 111°44.753'W
{3} 34°59.310'N; 111°44.879'W
{4} 34°59.772'N; 111°44.942'W
{5} 35°00.154'N; 111°45.603'W
{6} 35°00.158'N; 111°45.768'W
{7} 35°00.106'N; 111°46.017'W

N

West Fork Trail (Magnified)

{4}
Elev 5360 ft

Elev 5325 ft   To Flagstaff

P

{1}

Elev 5315 ft {3}   {2}
Elev 5315 ft

89A

Oak Creek

"Y"

89A

To Cottonwood

179

To I-17

Trail type	In-out
Challenge level	Moderate
Hiking distance (total)	7.2 miles
Cumulative ascent	750 feet

West Fork Trail   Elevation Profile

Elevation (ft)

5600

5500

5400

5300

0.0 0.5 1.0 1.5 2.0 2.5 3.0 3.5 4.0 4.5 5.0 5.5 6.0 6.5 7.2

Distance (mi)

Wilson Canyon Trail ★

Summary: A pleasant in-out hike in a shaded canyon with limited red rock views

Challenge Level: Moderate

Hiking Distance: About 1.3 miles each way or 2.6 miles round trip

Hiking Time: About 2 hours round trip

Trail Popularity:

Trailhead Directions: From the "Y" roundabout (see page 5), drive north on SR 89A to Midgley Bridge. The trailhead parking is on your left just after you cross the bridge {1}. The parking area can fill up quickly on the weekends. There is a toilet near the parking area.

Description: The trail begins away from SR 89A at the far end of the parking area, just beyond the picnic table pavilion. In about 100 feet, just past the toilet, you'll come to a metal sign for the Wilson Mountain (South) Trail on the right {2}. Continue straight ahead for about 0.1 mile then bear right at the fork in the trail and the signpost {3}. At first, the trail is wide but narrows further on. At about 0.5 mile, you'll come to a second, wooden sign for the Wilson Mountain Trail on the right {4}. You'll intersect the end of the Jim Thompson Trail in another 300 feet {5}.

The Wilson Canyon Trail crosses the wash at the bottom of the canyon 13 times as it winds back and forth for 1.3 miles. You'll be hiking among scrub oak and small Arizona cypress. The trail becomes somewhat narrow with large drop offs about 1 mile in.

After 1.3 miles, you'll come to a 3 foot tall cairn (and is the only cairn you'll find after passing the Jim Thompson Trail {5}) that sometimes has a sign End of

Trail on it marking the end of the official trail. Stop here or continue up the wash for another 75 feet. Watch for a steep side trail on your right {6}. Scramble up onto the nearby rock outcropping for some terrific views all around {7}. About 20 paces beyond the cairn, you'll see what looks like a continuation of the trail. But it only goes 50 feet or so then drops back into the wash.

Color Photos: Scan the QR code for color photos of this trail

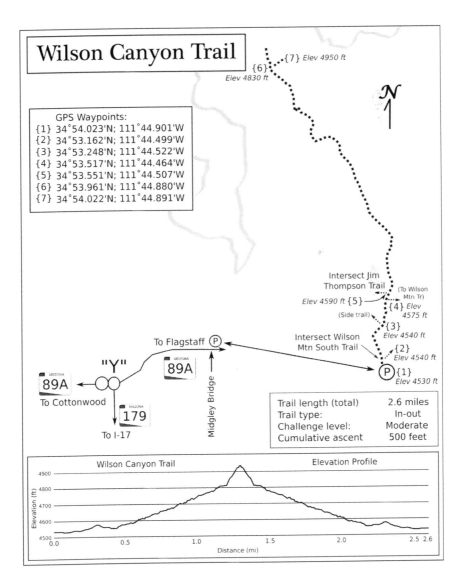

Wilson Canyon Trail

{7} Elev 4950 ft
{6}
Elev 4830 ft

N

GPS Waypoints:
{1} 34°54.023'N; 111°44.901'W
{2} 34°53.162'N; 111°44.499'W
{3} 34°53.248'N; 111°44.522'W
{4} 34°53.517'N; 111°44.464'W
{5} 34°53.551'N; 111°44.507'W
{6} 34°53.961'N; 111°44.880'W
{7} 34°54.022'N; 111°44.891'W

Intersect Jim
Thompson Trail   (To Wilson
                       Mtn Tr)
Elev 4590 ft {5}   {4} Elev
   (Side trail)   4575 ft
                      {3}
Intersect Wilson   Elev 4540 ft
Mtn South Trail   {2}
                       Elev 4540 ft
To Flagstaff (P)   (P){1}
                       Elev 4530 ft

"Y"
89A   89A

To Cottonwood
        179
To I-17

Midgley Bridge

Trail length (total)	2.6 miles
Trail type:	In-out
Challenge level:	Moderate
Cumulative ascent	500 feet

Wilson Canyon Trail   Elevation Profile

Elevation (ft): 4900, 4800, 4700, 4600, 4500
Distance (mi): 0.0, 0.5, 1.0, 1.5, 2.0, 2.5 2.6

Wilson Mountain North Trail

Summary: A hike up the north face of Wilson Mountain, the highest peak in the Sedona area

Challenge Level:
Hard

Hiking Distance:
2.25 miles each way to a view of Sedona or 4.5 miles round trip; 3.8 miles each way to the Sedona Overlook or 7.6 miles round trip

Hiking Time:
About 5 hours to the Sedona Overlook round trip

Trail Popularity: 🚶🚶

Trailhead Directions: From the "Y" roundabout (see page 5), drive north on SR 89A for 5.3 miles to the Encinoso Picnic Area. Turn left into the parking lot.

Description: After parking at the Encinoso Picnic Area {1}, walk north past the entrance drive. You'll see two parking spots in front of you. The trail begins in front of those two parking spots. In about 100 feet, you'll come to the sign that says, Trail 123 Wilson North. Continue parallel to SR 89A, in about 200 feet you make a left turn then begin gently climbing. You'll be hiking through a ponderosa pine forest. In 0.4 mile, you'll come to a sign indicating you are entering the Red Rock Secret Mountain Wilderness. After 1 mile {2}, the trail becomes narrow with a steep drop off for another 0.5 mile. After 1.8 miles, you'll come to the edge of the first bench of Wilson Mountain {3}. If you look to the north, you'll see the San Francisco Peaks in Flagstaff in the distance. Continue across the large open area to intersect the Wilson Mountain South Trail at a sign post, which is 2.25 miles from the parking area {4}. If you hike a few hundred feet south, you'll have a nice view of Sedona below {5}. You can begin the return trip here for a 4.5 mile hike.

Or, return to the signpost {4} then follow the Wilson Mountain Trail to the northwest. You'll steadily climb then after another 1.2 miles, you'll come to a sign and a fork in the trail {6}. If you go to the right, you'll be going to the Boynton Canyon Overlook, about 2 miles to the northwest. If you go to the left, you'll be hiking to the Sedona Overlook. You'll see the remains of a tool shed, which contained fire-fighting tools at one time. Vandals have pretty much destroyed the shed. You'll need to climb over fallen trees for the first 0.1 mile.

Follow the trail for 0.4 mile to the edge of Wilson Mountain {7} for a view of Sedona similar to that from the view at waypoint {5}.

Color Photos: Scan the QR code for color photos of this trail

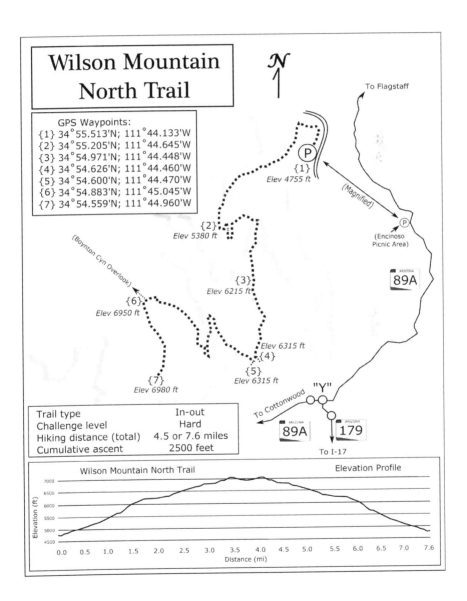

Wilson Mountain
North Trail

N

To Flagstaff

GPS Waypoints:
{1} 34°55.513'N; 111°44.133'W
{2} 34°55.205'N; 111°44.645'W
{3} 34°54.971'N; 111°44.448'W
{4} 34°54.626'N; 111°44.460'W
{5} 34°54.600'N; 111°44.470'W
{6} 34°54.883'N; 111°45.045'W
{7} 34°54.559'N; 111°44.960'W

P

{1}
Elev 4755 ft

(Magnified)

P
(Encinoso Picnic Area)

{2}
Elev 5380 ft

ARIZONA
89A

(Boynton Cyn Overlook)

{3}
Elev 6215 ft

{6}
Elev 6950 ft

Elev 6315 ft
{4}

{5}
Elev 6315 ft

{7}
Elev 6980 ft

"Y"

To Cottonwood

ARIZONA
89A

ARIZONA
179

To I-17

Trail type	In-out
Challenge level	Hard
Hiking distance (total)	4.5 or 7.6 miles
Cumulative ascent	2500 feet

Wilson Mountain North Trail   Elevation Profile

Elevation (ft)

7000
6500
6000
5500
5000
4500

0.0 0.5 1.0 1.5 2.0 2.5 3.0 3.5 4.0 4.5 5.0 5.5 6.0 6.5 7.0 7.6
Distance (mi)

Woods Canyon Trail

Summary: A sunny in-out hike along Dry Beaver Creek

Challenge Level: Moderate

Hiking Distance: About 2.5 miles each way or 5 miles round trip

Hiking Time: About 3 hours round trip

Trail Popularity: 🚶‍♂️

Trailhead Directions: From the "Y" roundabout (see page 5), drive south on SR 179 about 8.75 miles then turn left into the Red Rock Ranger Station {1}. Follow the drive a short distance then turn right at the first road rather than following the road to the left to the Visitor Center. Make a left then a right turn into the parking lot ahead. The trailhead is at the far south end of the parking area {2}.

Description: Just after you begin the trail, you will go through a gate then cross a small ditch, which always seems to have water in it. You'll shortly come to a second gate {3}. The trail becomes very rocky as it proceeds up a canyon and follows the path of Dry Beaver Creek.

You'll cross a wash after 1 mile {4}. After about 2 miles, you'll pass through a third gate {5} and soon intersect the Hot Loop Trail {6}. Continue straight on the Woods Canyon Trail for another 0.3 mile then make a right turn to go down

142

to Dry Beaver Creek {7}. Here you'll see large river rocks, which are deposited when Dry Beaver Creek floods {8}. The creek usually flows in the springtime because of the snow melt from the north. We usually stop here, but the trail continues on for about 12 miles, eventually ending at Interstate 17. It becomes more difficult the further you go. Wildflowers are in abundance in April most years. What little shade there is on this trail begins about 1.6 miles into the hike so this is a hot hike in the summer.

Color Photos: Scan the QR code for color photos of this trail

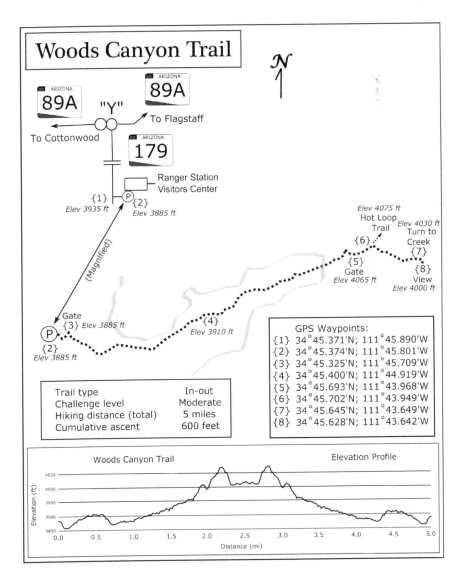

Woods Canyon Trail

N

ARIZONA
89A

"Y"

ARIZONA
89A

To Flagstaff

To Cottonwood

ARIZONA
179

Ranger Station
Visitors Center

{1}
Elev 3935 ft

P

{2}
Elev 3885 ft

(Magnified)

Gate
{3} *Elev 3885 ft*

P

{2}
Elev 3885 ft

{4}
Elev 3910 ft

Elev 4075 ft
Hot Loop
Trail
{6}

Elev 4030 ft
Turn to
Creek
{7}

{5}
Gate
Elev 4065 ft

{8}
View
Elev 4000 ft

GPS Waypoints:	
{1}	34°45.371'N; 111°45.890'W
{2}	34°45.374'N; 111°45.801'W
{3}	34°45.325'N; 111°45.709'W
{4}	34°45.400'N; 111°44.919'W
{5}	34°45.693'N; 111°43.968'W
{6}	34°45.702'N; 111°43.949'W
{7}	34°45.645'N; 111°43.649'W
{8}	34°45.628'N; 111°43.642'W

Trail type	In-out
Challenge level	Moderate
Hiking distance (total)	5 miles
Cumulative ascent	600 feet

Woods Canyon Trail | Elevation Profile

Elevation (ft)

Distance (mi)

Sedona Average Weather & Sunrise/Sunset Data

	Temperature (°F)		Precipitation	Sunrise	Sunset
	High	Low	(Inches)	(1st of	Month)
January	56	30	2.10	7:32 AM	5:30 PM
February	60	33	2.16	7:24 AM	5:58 PM
March	65	37	2.47	6:57 AM	6:24 PM
April	73	42	1.16	6:16 AM	6:48 PM
May	82	49	0.71	5:40 AM	7:10 PM
June	93	58	0.36	5:19 AM	7:32 PM
July	97	64	1.65	5:21 AM	7:42 PM
August	94	63	1.90	5:40 AM	7:29 PM
September	88	58	1.94	6:02 AM	6:55 PM
October	77	48	1.67	6:22 AM	6:14 PM
November	64	36	1.38	6:46 AM	5:37 PM
December	57	31	1.51	7:14 AM	5:20 PM
Average	75	46	1.50		

Vortex Information

If you come to Sedona with the thought of visiting a vortex or two, you are not alone. It's estimated that more than half of Sedona visitors are interested in experiencing the power of vortexes (vortices). There are four main Sedona vortexes: Airport Mesa, Bell Rock, Boynton Canyon, and Cathedral Rock. All four locations are described in this guidebook. We suggest that you approach each vortex without preconceived ideas of what you may experience and just let the experience happen. If nothing else, you'll enjoy some of Sedona's finest views. And, if you'd like additional information on the four main vortexes, plus information on the location of 10 additional power spots where vortex energy has been reported, you might be interested in our *Hiking the Vortexes* book that is available at many Sedona retailers or scan the code below.

GPS Data

When you read the trail descriptions, you will find numbers in curly brackets such as {1}, {2} and so on. These numbers refer to the GPS waypoints in the maps below each of the trail descriptions. In addition, elevation data for each of the GPS coordinates are shown on the maps as well as cumulative ascent data (total distance you'll climb on the hike). Specific GPS data, including tracks in the universal gpx format for all the trails contained in this guidebook are available at: https://greatsedonahikes.com/gps/gps.html or scan the code below.

Required Parking Pass

If you park in the National Forest around Sedona, you may need to display a Recreation Pass. If you park on private property or stop temporarily in the National Forest to take a photo remaining near your vehicle, you do not need to display a Recreation Pass.

A Recreation Pass is required for trailhead parking at many of the trails listed in this guide. It is also required for the Bootlegger, Banjo Bill, Halfway and Encinoso picnic areas in Oak Creek Canyon. Additionally, there are 3 special fee areas: Crescent Moon Ranch/Red Rock Crossing, West Fork Trail, and Grasshopper Point Picnic Area. Each area charges a separate, unique fee.

A Recreation Pass is: 1) A National Parks Pass, also known as a Federal Interagency Annual Pass 2) A Senior Pass, also known as a Federal Interagency Senior Pass issued to U.S. residents 62 years of age and older 3) A Federal Interagency Access Pass issued to individuals with permanent disabilities 4) A Red Rock Pass (described below).

If you do not have any of the above Federal Interagency Passes, you may display a Red Rock Pass, available for sale at many Sedona-area businesses, the Red Rock Ranger Station Visitor Center, the Sedona Chamber of Commerce Uptown Visitor Center and selected trailheads. The machines located at the trailheads only accept credit cards.

The Red Rock Pass is available as a $5 Daily Pass, a $15 Weekly Pass, a $20 Annual Pass, or a $40 Grand Annual Pass.

- The $5 Daily Red Rock Pass permits you to park in the National Forest as described above for the day of issue. It expires at midnight. It <u>does not include</u> the additional parking fees at the 3 special fee areas.
- The $15 Weekly Red Rock Pass permits you to park in the National Forest as described above for 7 days. It <u>does not include</u> the additional parking fees at the 3 special fee areas.
- The $20 Annual Red Rock Pass permits you to park in the National Forest as described above for 1 year. It <u>does not include</u> the additional parking fees at the 3 special fee areas.
- The $40 Grand Annual Pass permits you to park in the National Forest as described above and <u>includes</u> the additional parking fees at the 3 special fee areas for 1 year. It is available at the Red Rock Ranger Station and the Chamber's Uptown Visitor Center.

Because the Red Rock Pass Program changes periodically, check http://www.fs.usda.gov/main/coconino/passes-permits/recreation or scan the code below for the latest information.

Alphabetical List of Included Hiking Trails/Loop Hikes

★ symbol indicates Favorite Trail/Loop

Alphabetical List of Included Hiking Trails/Loop Hikes (Cont'd)

★ symbol indicates Favorite Trail/Loop

Alphabetical List of Included Hiking Trails/Loop Hikes (Cont'd)

List of 20 Favorite HikingTrails/Loop Hikes

★ symbol indicates Favorite Trail/Loop

Hiking Trails/Loop Hikes Listed By Difficulty

Easy

Airport Vortex	8
Baby Bell	88
Bail	90
Bell Rock Climb and Vortex	16
Bell Rock Loop	18
Boynton Canyon Vortex	24
Chapel	86
Chimney Rock Lower Loop	38
Chimney Rock Upper Loop	40
Coconino	118
Coffeepot	50
Cow Pies	58
Crusty	122
Fay Canyon (not to arch)	66
Hermit	118
Honanki Heritage Site	72
Llama/Baby Bell Loop	88
Llama/Bail Loop	90
Palatki Heritage Site	72
Rector Connector	18
Slim Shady	118
Slim Shady/Hermit Loop	118
Tabletop	8
Yucca	34

Easy to Moderate

Dry Creek	64
Fay Canyon (to the arch)	66
Jordan	82
Kelly Canyon	84
Llama	90
Marg's Draw	94
Pyramid Loop	104
Vultee Arch	134

Moderate

Adobe Jack	122
Adobe Jack/Javelina Loop	122
Aerie	6
Airport Loop	8
Baldwin Loop	10
Bear Sign	14
Bell Rock Pathway	20
Bell Rock Pathway/Templeton Loop	20
Bell-Weir	22
Boynton Canyon	24
Brins Mesa	26
Brins Mesa Overlook	28
Brins Mesa/Soldier Pass Loop	30
Broken Arrow	32

Broken Arrow/Submarine Loop	32
Canyon of Fools	34
Canyon of Fools/Mescal Loop	34
Carroll Canyon	102
Chuckwagon In-Out	42
Chuckwagon Loop	44
Cibola Pass	46
Cibola Pass/Jordan Loop	46
Cockscomb	48
Cockscomb/Aerie Loop	48
Courthouse Butte Loop	54
Courthouse Butte Short Loop	56
Devil's Bridge	60
Doe Mountain	62
Easy Breezy	76
Grand Central	124
Grand Central/Javelina Loop	124
Hangover In-Out	68
Herkenham	116
HiLine	70
HS Canyon	74
HT	76
HT/Easy Breezy Loop	76
Huckaby	78
Javelina	122
Jim Thompson	80
Little Horse	86
Llama/Little Horse Loop	90
Long Canyon	92
Mayan Maiden	96
Mescal	98
Mescal/Long Canyon Loop	98
Munds Wagon	100
Old Post	102
Old Post/Carroll Canyon Loop	102
Power Line Plunge	122
Rabbit Ears	106
Schuerman Mountain	108
Scorpion	110
Secret Canyon	112
Sedona View	8
Sky Walker	116
Sky Walker/Herkenham Loop	116
Soldier Pass	120
Sugarloaf	128
Templeton	132
West Fork	136
Wilson Canyon	138
Woods Canyon	142

149

Hiking Trails/Loop Hikes Listed By Difficulty (Cont'd)
Hard

Bear Mountain	12	Harding Springs	52
Cathedral Rock and Vortex	36	Secret Canyon/Bear Sign Loop	114
Cookstove to Harding Springs	52	Sterling Pass to Vultee Arch	126
David Miller	114	Telephone	130
Hangover/Munds Wagon Loop	68	Wilson Mountain North	140

Hiking Trails/Loop Hikes Listed By Feature

To/Near Arches

Devil's Bridge	60
Fay Canyon	66
Soldier Pass	120
Vultee Arch	134

Vortex Areas

Airport Vortex	8
Bell Rock Climb and Vortex	16
Boynton Canyon Vortex	24
Cathedral Rock Vortex	36

Indian Ruins

Boynton Canyon	24
Honanki Heritage Site	72
Palatki Heritage Site	72

To/Near Water

Baldwin Loop	10
Bell-Weir	22
Huckaby	78
Munds Wagon (spring runoff)	100
Templeton	132
West Fork	136
Woods Canyon (spring runoff)	142

Shaded Hiking Trails/Loop Hikes for Hot Weather

The following trails provide partial shade and may be suitable for summer hiking. But be sure to take extra water when hiking in the summer.

Bear Sign	14	Long Canyon (after 1 mile)	92
Boynton Canyon	24	Munds Wagon	100
Cibola Pass	46	Sterling Pass	126
Cookstove to Harding Springs	52	Telephone	130
Devil's Bridge	60	Vultee Arch	134
Dry Creek	64	West Fork	136
HS Canyon	74	Wilson Canyon	138
Kelly Canyon	84		

Hiking Trails/Loop Hikes for Muddy Conditions

After rain or snow, the following trails may be suitable for hiking. Do not hike if thunderstorm, lightning or flash flood warnings are present. Drizzles can quickly turn into electrical storms.

Baldwin Loop	10	Little Horse	86
Boynton Canyon	24	Llama	90
Courthouse Butte Loop	54	Marg's Draw	94
Courthouse Butte Short Loop	56	Schuerman Mountain	108
Doe Mountain	62	Templeton	132
Fay Canyon	66	Wilson Canyon	138
Jim Thompson	80		

Alphabetical List of Included Loop Hikes

Loop	Challenge Level	Page
Adobe Jack/Javelina Loop	Moderate	122
Airport Loop	Moderate	8
Baldwin Loop	Moderate	10
Bell Rock Loop	Easy	18
Bell Rock Pathway/Templeton Loop	Moderate	20
Brins Mesa/Soldier Pass Loop	Moderate	30
Broken Arrow/Submarine Rock Loop	Moderate	32
Canyon of Fools/Mescal Loop	Easy/Moderate	34
Chimney Rock Lower Loop	Easy	38
Chimney Rock Upper Loop	Easy	40
Chuckwagon Loop	Moderate	44
Cibola Pass/Jordan Loop	Moderate	46
Cockscomb/Aerie Loop	Moderate	48
Courthouse Butte Loop	Moderate	54
Courthouse Butte Short Loop	Moderate	56
Grand Central/Javelina Loop	Moderate	124
Hangover/Munds Wagon Loop	Hard	68
HT/Easy Breezy Loop	Moderate	76
Llama/Baby Bell Loop	Easy	88
Llama/Bail Loop	Moderate	90
Llama/Little Horse Loop	Moderate	90
Mescal/Long Canyon Loop	Moderate	98
Old Post/Carroll Canyon Loop	Moderate	102
Pyramid Loop	Moderate	104
Secret Canyon/Bear Sign Loop	Hard	114
Skywalker/Herkenham Loop	Moderate	116
Slim Shady/Hermit Loop	Moderate	118

Master Hiking Trail/Loop Hike Locator

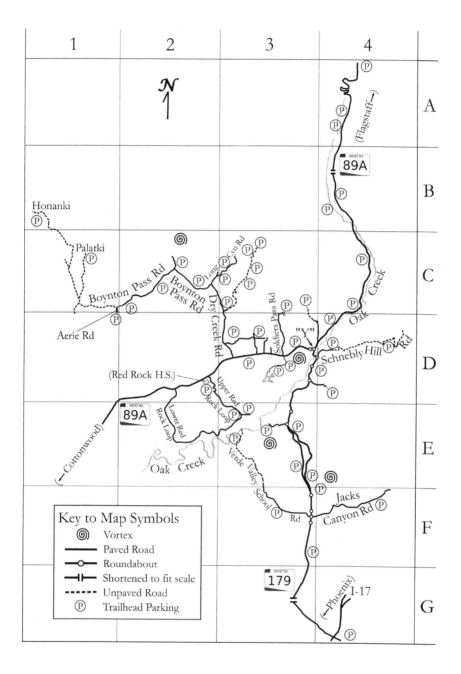

| | 1 | 2 | 3 | 4 | |

Key to Map Symbols
- Vortex
- Paved Road
- Roundabout
- Shortened to fit scale
- Unpaved Road
- Trailhead Parking

Index

Other Titles by the Authors

Hiking the Vortexes, Black & White Edition

Hiking the Vortexes, Color Edition

Hiking Record

Here's a page to record the name of the trail, the date you hiked it and notes from your hike. We'd appreciate any comments you'd like to share by emailing us at hikebook@greatsedonahikes.com

Name of Trail	Date Hiked	Comments/Notes

Made in the USA
Columbia, SC
13 July 2018